BAPTISTWAY ADULT BIBLE STUDY GUIDE®
LARGE PRINT EDITION

Profiles in Character
FROM THE EXODUS THROUGH THE RETURN FROM EXILE

DIANNE SWAIM
DON RANEY
ROBERT PRINCE
AUBREY KNOX
VIVIAN CONRAD

BAPTISTWAYPRESS®
Dallas, Texas

Profiles in Character: From the Exodus Through the Return from Exile—BaptistWay Adult Bible Study Guide®—Large Print

Copyright © 2011 by BAPTISTWAY PRESS®.
All rights reserved.
Printed in the United States of America.

No part of this book may be used or reproduced in any manner whatsoever without written permission except in the case of brief quotations. For information, contact BAPTISTWAY PRESS, Baptist General Convention of Texas, 333 North Washington, Dallas, TX 75246-1798.

BAPTISTWAY PRESS® is registered in U.S. Patent and Trademark Office.

Scripture marked NRSV is taken from the New Revised Standard Version Bible, copyright 1989, Division of Christian Education of the National Council of the Churches of Christ in the United States of America. Used by permission. All rights reserved. Unless otherwise indicated, all Scripture quotations in "Introducing Profiles in Character: From the Exodus Through the Return from Exile" and in lessons 1–4 are from the New Revised Standard Version Bible.

Scripture marked NASB is taken from the 1995 update of the New American Standard Bible®, Copyright © The Lockman Foundation 1960, 1962, 1963, 1968, 1971, 1972, 1973, 1975, 1977, 1995.
Used by permission. Unless otherwise indicated, all Scripture quotations in lessons 5–8 are from the New American Standard Bible.

Scripture marked NIV is taken from The Holy Bible, New International Version (North American Edition), copyright © 1973, 1978, 1984 by the International Bible Society. Used by permission of Zondervan Publishing House.
Unless otherwise indicated, all Scripture quotations in lessons 9–15 are from the New International Version.

BAPTISTWAY PRESS® Leadership Team
Associate Executive Director, Baptist General Convention of Texas: Steve Vernon
Director, Education/Discipleship Center: Chris Liebrum
Director, Bible Study/Discipleship Team: Phil Miller
Publisher, BAPTISTWAY PRESS®: Ross West

Cover and Interior Design and Production: Desktop Miracles, Inc.
Printing: Data Reproductions Corporation

First edition: May 2011
ISBN-13: 978-1-934731-71-0

How to Make the Best Use of This Issue

Whether you're the teacher or a student—

1. Start early in the week before your class meets.

2. Overview the study. Review the table of contents and read the study introduction. Try to see how each lesson relates to the overall study.

3. Use your Bible to read and consider prayerfully the Scripture passages for the lesson. (You'll see that each writer has chosen a favorite translation for the lessons in this issue. You're free to use the Bible translation you prefer and compare it with the translation chosen for that unit, of course.)

4. After reading all the Scripture passages in your Bible, then read the writer's comments. The comments are intended to be an aid to your study of the Bible.

5. Read the small articles—"sidebars"—in each lesson. They are intended to provide additional, enrichment information and inspiration and to encourage thought and application.

6. Try to answer for yourself the questions included in each lesson. They're intended to encourage further

thought and application, and they can also be used in the class session itself.

If you're the teacher—

A. Do all of the things just mentioned, of course. As you begin the study with your class, be sure to find a way to help your class know the date on which each lesson will be studied. You might do this in one or more of the following ways:

- In the first session of the study, briefly overview the study by identifying with your class the date on which each lesson will be studied. Lead your class to write the date in the table of contents on page 9 and on the first page of each lesson.

- Make and post a chart that indicates the date on which each lesson will be studied.

- If all of your class has e-mail, send them an e-mail with the dates the lessons will be studied.

- Provide a bookmark with the lesson dates. You may want to include information about your church and then use the bookmark as an outreach tool, too. A model for a bookmark can be downloaded from www.baptistwaypress.org on the Resources for Adults page.

- Develop a sticker with the lesson dates, and place it on the table of contents or on the back cover.

HOW TO *Make the Best Use of This Issue* 5

B. Get a copy of the *Teaching Guide*, a companion piece to this *Study Guide*. The *Teaching Guide* contains additional Bible comments plus two teaching plans. The teaching plans in the *Teaching Guide* are intended to provide practical, easy-to-use teaching suggestions that will work in your class.

C. After you've studied the Bible passage, the lesson comments, and other material, use the teaching suggestions in the *Teaching Guide* to help you develop your plan for leading your class in studying each lesson.

D. Teaching resource items for use as handouts are available free at www.baptistwaypress.org.

E. You may want to get the additional adult Bible study comments—*Adult Online Bible Commentary*—by Dr. Jim Denison (president, The Center for Informed Faith, and theologian-in-residence, Baptist General Convention of Texas). Call 1–866–249–1799 or e-mail baptistway@texasbaptists.org to order *Adult Online Bible Commentary*. It is available only in electronic format (PDF) from our website. The price of these comments is $6 for individuals and $25 for a group of five. A church or class that participates in our advance order program for free shipping can receive *Adult Online Bible Commentary* free. Call 1–866–249–1799 or see www.baptistwaypress.org to purchase or for information on participating in our free shipping program for the next study.

F. Additional teaching plans are also available in electronic format (PDF) by calling 1–866–249–1799. The price of these additional teaching plans is $5 for an individual and $20 for a group of five. A church or class that participates in our advance order program for free shipping can receive *Adult Online Teaching Plans* free. Call 1–866–249–1799 or see www.baptistwaypress.org for information on participating in our free shipping program for the next study.

G. You also may want to get the enrichment teaching help that is provided on the internet by the *Baptist Standard* at www.baptiststandard.com. (Other class participants may find this information helpful, too.) Call 214–630–4571 to begin your subscription to the printed or electronic edition of the *Baptist Standard*.

H. Enjoy leading your class in discovering the meaning of the Scripture passages and in applying these passages to their lives.

Writers of This Study Guide

Dianne Swaim, writer of lessons one through four, lives with her husband Gordon and son David in North Little Rock, Arkansas. She is a member of Second Baptist Church in Little Rock. She coordinates the chaplaincy department as the Spiritual Care Manager of Arkansas Hospice. She also serves as a chaplain for the Veterans Administration, which gives her a special opportunity to minister to veterans. She is a graduate of Southwestern Baptist Theological Seminary (M.Div.), Fort Worth, Texas. Together she and Gordon have three children and nine grandchildren.

Don Raney wrote lessons five through eight. Dr. Raney is pastor of First Baptist Church, Petersburg, Texas. He is a graduate of the University of Alabama (B.A.) and received his Ph.D. in Old Testament from Southwestern Baptist Theological Seminary.

Robert Prince, writer of lessons nine through eleven, serves as senior pastor of First Baptist Church, Waynesville, North Carolina. A native of Georgia, Dr. Prince has also served in pastorates in that state and in Texas. He has also served as an adjunct instructor at Southwestern and New Orleans Baptist Theological Seminaries, and at Wayland

Baptist University. He earned his B.A. degree from Baylor University, and his M.Div. and Ph.D. degrees from Southwestern Baptist Theological Seminary.

Aubrey Knox wrote lessons twelve and thirteen. He is minister of education and administration for First Baptist Church, Lufkin, Texas. After graduating with a B.A. from Houston Baptist College, Aubrey received his M.Div. from Southwestern Baptist Theological Seminary. He has served churches in Ganado, Missouri City, Houston, and Livingston, all in Texas. He is married to Janice, and they have two grown children, Kevin Knox and Julie Johnson, who live in the Austin area. Aubrey enjoys golf and officiates Texas high school football.

Vivian Conrad is the writer of lessons fourteen and fifteen in this *Study Guide* and of the teaching plans for these two lessons in the *Teaching Guide*. She and her husband recently moved back to the United States after twenty-four years overseas, during the last eleven of which she taught Bible at Faith Academy, an international school in the Philippines for children of missionaries. Vivian holds the degrees of Bachelor of Arts in Christian Education from Dallas Baptist University and the Master of Arts in Theology from Southwestern Seminary. She teaches Sunday School and is Discipleship Director at First Baptist Church, Mineral Wells, Texas.

Profiles in Character: From the Exodus Through the Return from Exile

How to Make the Best Use of This Issue	3
Writers for This Study Guide	7
Introducing Profiles in Character: From the Exodus Through the Return from Exile	11
Chart: Profiles in Character: Personalities in the Old Testament from the Exodus Through the Return from Exile	16

DATE OF STUDY

LESSON 1	_____	*Women at Moses' Birth: Taking Action to Help Children* EXODUS 1:15—2:10	18
LESSON 2	_____	*Moses: Seeking Good for Undeserving People* EXODUS 32:7–14, 30–34	32
LESSON 3	_____	*Caleb: Showing Courageous Faith* NUMBERS 13:25—14:10A	46
LESSON 4	_____	*The Sisterhood: Challenging Unfairness* NUMBERS 27:1–11	60
LESSON 5	_____	*Joshua: Leading in Following God* JOSHUA 24:1–3A, 13–27	74
LESSON 6	_____	*Deborah: Exercising Strong Leadership* JUDGES 4:1–16; 5:1–7	88

LESSON 7	_____	Samuel: Being Faithful to the Highest Allegiance
		1 Samuel 12:1–5, 13–25 102
LESSON 8	_____	David and Nathan: Accepting Personal Responsibility for Sin
		2 Samuel 11:2–15; 12:1–13a 116
LESSON 9	_____	Amos: Facing Opposition Courageously
		Amos 1:1–2; 2:6–16; 7:10–17 130
LESSON 10	_____	Micaiah: Telling the Hard Truth
		1 Kings 22:6–28 146
LESSON 11	_____	Huldah: Interpreting and Proclaiming God's Message
		2 Chronicles 34:19–31 162
LESSON 12	_____	Jeremiah: Being Faithful in the Depths of Despair
		Jeremiah 20:7–18; 26:1–15 176
LESSON 13	_____	Shadrach, Meshach, and Abednego: Giving Unlimited Devotion to God
		Daniel 3 192
LESSON 14	_____	Esther: Taking the Ultimate Risk
		Esther 4:1–16 208
LESSON 15	_____	Nehemiah: Standing Up for People
		Nehemiah 2:1–5; 5:1–13 222

Our Next New Study   237
Additional Future Adult Bible Studies   238
How to Order More Bible Study Materials   239

Introducing

PROFILES IN CHARACTER: *From the Exodus Through the Return from Exile*

We learn much about life and how to live it through knowing people. People who provide examples both good and bad help us to put flesh and blood on principles and teachings. We often decide to travel the road to the highest and best in life not simply because an idea or ideal seems desirable but because we have seen someone we respect follow that road, too. This is so from our earliest days of life, and it continues in adulthood. People are a never-ending source of learning. Even the truths of the Christian faith can seem dry, abstract, and hazy until we see them lived out, even though imperfectly, in real live human beings.

Personalities in the Bible

The Bible is a rich source of biographical information about how real live human beings have lived out their faith. A recent BaptistWay Bible study on Genesis—called *Genesis: People Relating to God*—focused on seven richly varied personalities in that book.[1] Now, in this study, we continue the journey through the Old Testament by considering what additional biblical personalities have to teach us.[2]

Some of these Old Testament personalities you likely have heard of and learned from previously. There's a good chance, though, that some of them have been skipped over in your study of the Bible and you've missed the insights their lives offer. It's time to learn about them and from them.

An Additional Purpose

This study of Old Testament personalities serves an additional purpose. These personalities are studied in chronological order through the Old Testament, from the Exodus through the return from Exile, a period of roughly 1,000 years. The intent is to set each lesson in the context of its era in Old Testament history and so help to provide a way for you to get a firmer grasp on the main events of the Old Testament and how selected biblical personalities fit into the sweep of Old Testament history.

Of course, each lesson can stand on its own, but the study will be richer if you will become conscious of where each personality fits within the Old Testament context. To provide further help in visualizing the entire study, a chart called "Profiles in Character: Personalities in the Old Testament from the Exodus Through the Return from Exile" is provided in this *Study Guide* on pages 16-17.

Selecting the Personalities for Study

The BaptistWay publishing schedule provided an opportunity to have fifteen lessons in this study. Many Old Testament personalities could have been studied, and you might well arrive at a different list of fifteen from the list in this study. Here are some of the factors in the choices of these fifteen lessons:

(1) Study people whose lives offer significant teachings to us

(2) Study at least one person from each Old Testament era

(3) Study the personalities in chronological order

(4) Study some characters who are less familiar and tend to be overlooked but who illuminate life perhaps in out-of-the-ordinary ways and thus have much to teach us

(5) Select people who can provide a variety of learnings

(6) Select characters who have not been studied recently (So, for example, because of the recent study in Genesis, no characters from Genesis were selected.)

PROFILES IN CHARACTER:
FROM THE EXODUS THROUGH THE RETURN FROM EXILE

Lesson 1	Women at Moses' Birth: Taking Action to Help Children	Exodus 1:15—2:10
Lesson 2	Moses: Seeking Good for Undeserving People	Exodus 32:7–14, 30–34
Lesson 3	Caleb: Showing Courageous Faith	Numbers 13:25—14:10a
Lesson 4	The Sisterhood: Challenging Unfairness	Numbers 27:1–11
Lesson 5	Joshua: Leading in Following God	Joshua 24:1–3a, 13–27
Lesson 6	Deborah: Exercising Strong Leadership	Judges 4:1–16; 5:1–7
Lesson 7	Samuel: Being Faithful to the Highest Allegiance	1 Samuel 12:1–5, 13–25
Lesson 8	David and Nathan: Accepting Personal Responsibility for Sin	2 Samuel 11:2–15; 12:1–13a
Lesson 9	Amos: Facing Opposition Courageously	Amos 1:1–2; 2:6–16; 7:10–17
Lesson 10	Micaiah: Telling the Hard Truth	1 Kings 22:6–28
Lesson 11	Huldah: Interpreting and Proclaiming God's Message	2 Chronicles 34:19–31
Lesson 12	Jeremiah: Being Faithful in the Depths of Despair	Jeremiah 20:7–18; 26:1–15
Lesson 13	Shadrach, Meshach, and Abednego: Giving Unlimited Devotion to God	Daniel 3
Lesson 14	Esther: Taking the Ultimate Risk	Esther 4:1–16
Lesson 15	Nehemiah: Standing Up for People	Nehemiah 2:1–5; 5:1–13

NOTES

1. *The Book of Genesis: People Relating to God* (Dallas, Texas: BaptistWay Press, 2010). For information and to order, see www.baptistwaypress.org, or call 1–866–249–1799.
2. Unless otherwise indicated, all Scripture quotations in "Introducing Profiles in Character: From the Exodus Through the Exile" are from the New Revised Standard Version.

Profiles in Character:
Personalities in the Old Testament from the Exodus Through the Return from Exile[1]

I. Creation and Early Records	II. The Patriarchs	III. The Exodus	IV. Wandering in the Wilderness and Entering the Promised Land	V. The Judges
prior to about 1750 B.C.	about 1750–1350 B.C.	about 1350–1250 B.C.	about 1300–1200 B.C.	about 1200–1020 B.C.
Books:				
Genesis 1—11	Genesis 12—50	Exodus	Numbers 13—36	Judges
		Leviticus	Deuteronomy	Ruth
		Numbers 1—12	Joshua	1 Samuel 1—12
People:				
Adam	Abraham	**Women at Moses' Birth (Lesson 1)**	Caleb (Lesson 3)	Deborah, Barak (Lesson 6)
Eve	Sarah		**The Sisterhood (Lesson 4)**	Gideon
Cain	Lot	**Moses (Lesson 2)**	Rahab	Samson
Abel	Isaac		**Joshua (Lesson 5)**	Ruth
Noah	Rebekah	Aaron		Hannah
	Jacob			**Samuel (Lesson 7)**
	Leah			
	Rachel			
	Joseph			

VI. The Kingdom	VII. The Divided Kingdom	VIII. Only Judah	IX. The Exile	X. Return from Exile
1020–922 B.C.	922–721 B.C.	721–587 B.C.	597–539 B.C.	539–333 B.C.
Books:				
1 Samuel 12—31	1 Kings 12—22;	2 Kings 17—25	Ezekiel	Ezra
2 Samuel	2 Kings 1—17	Isaiah 1—39	Isaiah 40—66	Haggai
1 Kings 1—12	Amos	Micah	Obadiah	Zechariah
1 Chronicles 10 — 2 Chronicles 9	Hosea	Jeremiah	2 Chronicles 36	Nehemiah
	Isaiah 1—39	Zephaniah		Malachi
	2 Chronicles 10—28	Nahum		2 Chronicles 36
		Habakkuk		
		2 Chronicles 29—36		
People:				
Saul	Kings of Israel and Judah 922–721 B.C.	Kings of Judah 721–587 B.C.	Ezekiel	Ezra
Jonathan		Micah	Daniel	**Nehemiah (Lesson 15)**
David, Bathsheba, Nathan (Lesson 8)	Elijah	Hezekiah	**Shadrach, Meshach, and Abednego (Lesson 13)**	Haggai
	Elisha	Josiah		Malachi
Solomon	**Amos (Lesson 9)**	**Huldah (Lesson 11)**	**Esther (Lesson 14)**	
	Micaiah (Lesson 10)	**Jeremiah (Lesson 12)**		
	Hosea			
	Isaiah			

NOTES

1. Bold type indicates people in lessons in this study.

FOCAL TEXT
Exodus 1:15—2:10

BACKGROUND
Exodus 1:1—2:10

LESSON ONE

Women at Moses' Birth:
Taking Action to Help Children

MAIN IDEA

Women acted boldly and courageously to overcome the pharaoh's evil plans and help children, including a special child.

QUESTION TO EXPLORE

What will you do to help children?

STUDY AIM

To summarize the ways in which the women at Moses' birth acted to help children and to identify ways I will take action to help children

QUICK READ

God used not one but five women to save both a generation of children and one special child, Moses.

An old African proverb that has become well-known states, *It takes a village to raise a child*. The origin of this proverb is not certain, but we can find the concept as far back as Egypt in the second millennium when five women followed God's leadership and risked their lives to save Hebrew children. Two of these women were instrumental in saving perhaps thousands of babies. The other three worked together to save the life of one. All of them took part in God's plan to raise this one child into a man who would lead God's people out of Egypt, through the wilderness, and into the Promised Land. His name was Moses.

Exodus 1:15–22

[15] The king of Egypt said to the Hebrew midwives, whose names were Shiphrah and Puah, [16] "When you help the Hebrew women in childbirth and observe them on the delivery stool, if it is a boy, kill him; but if it is a girl, let her live." [17] The midwives, however, feared God and did not do what the king of Egypt had told them to do; they let the boys live. [18] Then the king of Egypt summoned the midwives and asked them, "Why have you done this? Why have you let the boys live?" [19] The midwives answered Pharaoh, "Hebrew women are not like Egyptian women; they are vigorous and give birth before the midwives arrive." [20] So God was kind to the midwives and the people increased

LESSON 1: *Women at Moses' Birth*

and became even more numerous. **21** And because the midwives feared God, he gave them families of their own. **22** Then Pharaoh gave this order to all his people: "Every boy that is born you must throw into the Nile, but let every girl live."

EXODUS 2:1–10

1 Now a man of the house of Levi married a Levite woman, **2** and she became pregnant and gave birth to a son. When she saw that he was a fine child, she hid him for three months. **3** But when she could hide him no longer, she got a papyrus basket for him and coated it with tar and pitch. Then she placed the child in it and put it among the reeds along the bank of the Nile. **4** His sister stood at a distance to see what would happen to him. **5** Then Pharaoh's daughter went down to the Nile to bathe, and her attendants were walking along the river bank. She saw the basket among the reeds and sent her slave girl to get it. **6** She opened it and saw the baby. He was crying, and she felt sorry for him. "This is one of the Hebrew babies," she said. **7** Then his sister asked Pharaoh's daughter, "Shall I go and get one of the Hebrew women to nurse the baby for you?" **8** "Yes, go," she answered. And the girl went and got the baby's mother. **9** Pharaoh's daughter said to her, "Take this baby and nurse him for me, and I will pay you." So the woman took the baby and nursed him. **10** When the child grew older, she took him to Pharaoh's daughter and he became her son. She named him Moses, saying, "I drew him out of the water."

A Mandate to Kill (1:15–22)

The Book of Exodus opens with Egypt struggling over population growth among the Hebrews: "The Israelites were fruitful and prolific; they multiplied and grew exceedingly strong, so that the land was filled with them" (Exodus 1:7).[1] The crisis was not one of space or economics. Rather, its political ramifications caused concern. This explosion of Israelites caused Pharaoh to shudder at the thought of possible alliances by the Hebrews with an enemy in case of war. He had to get on top of this problem quickly.

Pharaoh's first approach was to wear down the Israelites. He appointed ruthless taskmasters over them. These taskmasters imposed tasks intended to hurt the slaves rather than help the masters. But Pharaoh underestimated the survival instinct and national pride of these Hebrew slaves: "The more they were oppressed, the more they multiplied and spread, so that the Egyptians came to dread the Israelites" (Exod. 1:12).

Pharaoh must have paced the floor at night thinking of a fail-proof plan to repress the growth of his slave populace. His first plan, to inflict pain, failed. His second was to reduce the birthrate of this ever-growing people group through infanticide. Little did he know, however, that he was about to draft two wise and courageous women to be his directors of death.

Midwives in biblical times served as *birth doctors.* Both Hebrew and Egyptian women alike gave birth on birthstools. Although there were probably different styles, a typical birthstool was composed of two stones on which the Hebrew women knelt to deliver their babies.[2] According to Ezekiel 16:4, a midwife's primary duty was to cut the umbilical cord, wash the infant, rub the baby with salt, and wrap it in cloths.

Pharaoh called in two midwives, who probably were the overseers of hundreds of midwives. When one considers the large number of Israelites, having only two midwives would have been unrealistic.

Puah and Shiphrah were Hebrew slaves themselves. Imagine how they must have felt when being called to appear before the most powerful man in the ancient world. They may have been nervous about their appearance before him, and they were likely horrified when given their command. Rather than bringing life into the world, they were directed to kill all male Hebrew babies at birth.

God intervened in this diabolical plan by placing two God-fearing women in the positions of lead midwives. Their minds must have raced with the realization of how many babies they were being mandated to kill. They knew they could not carry out Pharaoh's orders. Their higher authority was God. Overseeing the killing of babies was not an option. But what were their options? They knew their lives were at risk.

Their choice was brilliant. When the news came to Pharaoh that Hebrew baby boys were living, he called in Puah and Shiphrah and demanded an answer. They probably took advantage of a subject of which Pharaoh had neither knowledge nor experience: "The midwives said to Pharaoh, because the Hebrew women are not like the Egyptian women; for they are vigorous and give birth before the midwife comes to them" (Exod. 1:19). However, the midwives were spared death by Pharaoh and rewarded by God with families of their own.

In seeming desperation, Pharaoh then declared the most evil plan of all: "Every boy that is born to the Hebrews you shall throw into the Nile, but you shall let every girl live" (1:22). Two women had shown remarkable courage. A generation of Israelites had been saved. But two additional courageous women were about to be called into action.

A Plan to Save (2:1–4)

One might imagine the horror and heartbreak of Puah and Shiphrah upon learning of this desperate plan of Pharaoh. Risking their lives by lying to the king, they had saved hundreds, if not thousands, of baby boys. Now his new plan completely bypassed them. They could only protect the babies at birth. The cries of heartbroken mothers whose newborn sons were thrown into the Nile must have gone with them to their graves.

The women's courage had not been in vain, however, for out of this generation of Hebrew babies, God would bring the one who would lead the Israelites out of Egypt. But Pharaoh had erected yet another hurdle that must first be crossed. A devoted and determined mother, along with her daughter, would serve as God's agents in this victory.

No name is given for the mother of Moses in these verses, perhaps to emphasize the instincts and character of her motherhood rather than her personhood. In Exodus 6:20 and Numbers 26:59 she is named Jochebed. She came from the lineage of Levi's tribe and had married her brother Kohath's oldest son, Amram. Both of Moses' parents came from a priestly tribe, which may be why they both still worshiped God when most Hebrews had defected to the idols of the Egyptians (Ezekiel 20:6–8).

Jochebed and Amram had three children: Miriam, Aaron, and Moses. God would use all three for his salvation plan for the Israelites. This is the first time we see the courage of Miriam, but it would not be the last. She would accompany Moses and Aaron through the Exodus and serve as a leader of women in praise and worship of God.

We are not privy to any word from God to Jochebed about her newborn son's future. God certainly had a history of prophesying to fathers or mothers about the upcoming greatness of their sons. Examples include Abraham and Isaac (Genesis 17:19), Rebekah and Jacob (Gen. 25:23), and later Mary and Jesus (Luke 1:28–32). Scripture does say, however, that when she "saw that he was a fine baby" (Exod. 2:2), she hid him for three months. As with the midwives, her life was on the line should her baby be discovered.

Finding it impossible to hide an infant any longer from the prying eyes and ears of the Egyptians, Jochebed crafted a papyrus basket in which to place her son. The same word for "basket" in this story is the word for *ark* in the salvation story of Noah. Ironically, she carried out Pharaoh's edict: she cast her baby into the Nile. But as with Noah's family, the ark basket would save her son.

Much is left to speculation in this story. We do not know whether Jochebed intended to place Moses where the Pharaoh's daughter came to bathe. She may have intended only to hide him in the bulrushes during the day and return him to her bosom at night. Her plan did not matter as much as God's plan. In God's plan, Moses would be educated in the court of the very pharaoh who originally ordered his death.

A Son to Raise (2:5–10)

The last character in the miraculous plan to save Moses was a daughter of Pharaoh. Little could Pharaoh's daughter

LESSON 1: *Women at Moses' Birth*

have known what she would discover in her bathing spot that day. First she discovered the basket, perhaps because she heard the muffled cries of a baby emanating from it. She immediately recognized this baby as Hebrew and simultaneously must have realized the desperation of a loving mother. She probably put two and two together when a small girl suddenly appeared and offered to find the services of a nursemaid.

Courage begets courage. Perhaps Jochebed's courage inspired the same in this princess. To take a Hebrew child into the very court of this murderous pharaoh would require much courage.

Scripture does not tell us much about the transactions between this new adoptive mother and the birth mother. Much respect was required on both sides. The weaning of Moses from his mother would have taken anywhere from two to seven years. By that time, even if Pharaoh saw him, he would likely have ignored the child.

Lesson in Today's Life

The unborn and children of tender age cannot advocate for themselves. Neither can oppressed children of any age. They must have advocates.

All five of these women in Exodus took a stand for life. The midwives had the courage to advocate for unborn children of an entire nation. Jochebed, Miriam, and

Pharaoh's daughter advocated for the life of one small baby. Regardless of reasons for personal involvement, these women accepted the challenge.

Today we face similar challenges. They may confront us on an individual basis or under the umbrella of social justice. We cannot ignore the children who depend on us. They may belong to us or to an African woman in a small hut in Zimbabwe. They may be owned by a human slave traffic owner. Most importantly, they belong to God.

Puah, Shiphrah, Jochebed, Miriam, and Pharaoh's daughter took actions to preserve life. Can we do any less?

PHARAOH

An ancient pharaoh (king) was not only an absolute monarch, but he was also the supreme commander of the armies, chief justice of the royal court, and high priest of the nation's religion. His absolute power may be seen in that justice was defined as *what Pharaoh loves* and wrongdoing as *what Pharaoh hates*.[3] Because the dates of the Exodus are uncertain, with scholars holding various positions, so is the identity of the pharaoh of this Scripture passage. Some believe Ramses II was the ruling pharaoh; some believe Amenhotep I or Thutmose III ruled.[4] An interesting note is that the pharaoh remains nameless, while the names of the two ordinary midwives are given to be remembered throughout all history.

Two Models

- Green Acres Baptist Church in Tyler, Texas, adopted a program, *Hope for 100*. The goal was to have one hundred children adopted or fostered by church members. Within eighteen months they had exceeded their goal.[5] What variation of such a plan could your church do?

- Second Baptist Church in Little Rock, Arkansas, has an Adoption/Orphan Care Group. One of their projects is to support the local Department of Human Services as they take in children for home placement. They furnish snacks, toys, and other items to help the children feel comfortable as they wait to be placed.[6]

Questions

1. Puah and Shiphrah literally outwitted the Pharaoh by what we might call *creative disobedience*. Is this ever justified? How might this concept be called for today in defending children?

2. What credentials for leading the Israelites out of Egypt do you see Moses had as a result of having both a Hebrew home and an Egyptian home? See Acts 7:17–22. Can you see God's plan unfolding for this child?

3. The midwives and Moses' mother and sister had faith in God. Based on her background, Pharaoh's daughter probably did not. How and why would God use believers and unbelievers? How does God do that today?

4. If God convicted you to take one step today toward helping a helpless child (or children), what could you do?

NOTES

1. Unless otherwise indicated, all Scripture quotations in lessons 1–4 are from the New Revised Standard Version.
2. Walter A. Elwell, *Evangelical Commentary on the Bible* (Grand Rapids: Baker Book House, 1989), 41.
3. Trent C. Butler, General Editor, *Holman Bible Dictionary* (Nashville: Holman Bible Publishers, 1991), see "Pharaoh."
4. David S. Dockery, General Editor, *Holman Bible Handbook* (Nashville: Holman Bible Publishers, 1992), 144.
5. www.hopefor100.org. Accessed 1/3/2011.
6. www.2bclr.com. Accessed 1/3/2011.

FOCAL TEXT
Exodus 32:7–14, 30–34

BACKGROUND
Exodus 32

LESSON TWO

Moses:
SEEKING GOOD FOR
UNDESERVING PEOPLE

MAIN IDEA

Moses interceded with God for the good of the people even though they did not deserve it.

QUESTION TO EXPLORE

How shall we treat people who don't deserve to be treated well?

STUDY AIM

To analyze Moses' intercession with God for the people and identify actions to take toward people I know

QUICK READ

In Moses' absence the Israelites betrayed both him and God. He had the choice to turn away from them or turn to God on their behalf. He chose the latter.

Frank killed Mrs. Dais's husband.[1] He didn't mean to. He was crazy on drugs, and the aliens were telling him to get out of the city and kill every living creature. Before the police could get to him he had bludgeoned eight people, killing one. Mrs. Dais's husband died a few months later.

Frank was sentenced to thirty years in prison for manslaughter. Just before his transfer from jail to prison, Mrs. Dais paid Frank a visit. She sat before him, and with tears streaming down her face, said, "Frank, I want to hate you for what you did. But I'm a Christian and everything in my Bible tells me I have to forgive you. I've prayed for you, but I don't know how anything good could ever come out of this unless God makes you into a minister." With that, she handed him her husband's Bible! Extreme response to an extreme hurt? Absolutely. Did Frank deserve it? Absolutely not.

Even as Moses was standing in the presence of the living God, the Israelites were making revelry before a handmade idol. Moses was about to come face-to-face with an ungrateful, depraved, and rebellious group of people, people for whom he had risked his life. Did they deserve an intercession on their behalf? Absolutely not. Would Moses face an angry God on their behalf anyway? Absolutely.

Exodus 32:7–14, 30–34

7 Then the Lord said to Moses, "Go down, because your people, whom you brought up out of Egypt, have become corrupt. **8** They have been quick to turn away from what I commanded them and have made themselves an idol cast in the shape of a calf. They have bowed down to it and sacrificed to it and have said, 'These are your gods, O Israel, who brought you up out of Egypt.' **9** "I have seen these people," the Lord said to Moses, "and they are a stiff-necked people. **10** Now leave me alone so that my anger may burn against them and that I may destroy them. Then I will make you into a great nation." **11** But Moses sought the favor of the Lord his God. "O Lord," he said, "why should your anger burn against your people, whom you brought out of Egypt with great power and a mighty hand? **12** Why should the Egyptians say, 'It was with evil intent that he brought them out, to kill them in the mountains and to wipe them off the face of the earth'? Turn from your fierce anger; relent and do not bring disaster on your people. **13** Remember your servants Abraham, Isaac and Israel, to whom you swore by your own self: 'I will make your descendants as numerous as the stars in the sky and I will give your descendants all this land I promised them, and it will be their inheritance forever.'" **14** Then the Lord relented and did not bring on his people the disaster he had threatened.

• • • • • • • • • • • • • • • • • • • •

30 The next day Moses said to the people, "You have committed a great sin. But now I will go up to the Lord; perhaps I can make atonement for your sin." **31** So Moses went back to the Lord and said, "Oh, what a great sin these people have committed! They have made themselves gods of gold. **32** But now, please forgive their sin—but if not, then blot me out of the book you have written." **33** The Lord replied to Moses, "Whoever has sinned against me I will blot out of my book. **34** Now go, lead the people to the place I spoke of, and my angel will go before you. However, when the time comes for me to punish, I will punish them for their sin."

The People Without Moses (32:1–6)

God and Moses together led the Hebrews out of Egypt and delivered them from slavery. Three months after they left Egypt, they arrived at the wilderness of Sinai (Exodus 19:1). The first time God called Moses up to the mountain, Moses returned to the Hebrews soon thereafter. This time, however, he neither came down nor sent word. "As for this Moses, the man who brought us up out of the land of Egypt, we do not know what has become of him" (Exod. 32:1). As far as they knew, he either had died or abandoned them.

The Israelites had never been totally dedicated to God. While they said they were, even in Egypt many of them adopted the gods of their slave masters. Time after time they turned against Moses. They complained in Egypt, and they complained in the wilderness (Deuteronomy

9:7). Aaron and Hur, though, had stood strong in the past for Moses (Exod. 17:12–13). No doubt Moses felt safe leaving the people in their hands while he was on the mountain. Instead, he unknowingly left them in a leadership vacuum.

Many, if not most, scholars believe the golden calf that "came out" was originally intended to represent Yahweh. The calf image symbolized deity in the Near East. Years later, after the death of Solomon, the Israelites would once again worship calves of gold. "Here are your gods, O Israel, who brought you up out of the land of Egypt" (1 Kings 12:28). Whatever their intention, they now put another god before Yahweh. Aaron's poor excuse when Moses confronted him was not enough to spare him God's anger. "The Lord was so angry with Aaron that he was ready to destroy him, but I interceded also on behalf of Aaron at that same time" (Deut. 9:20).

Moses with God (32:7–14)

For forty days, Moses had received instructions from God. He must have been ecstatic with the final outcome of a covenant written with the very finger of God. Little could he have been prepared for the scene awaiting him at the foot of the mountain. But God knew. He said, "Go down at once! Your people, whom you brought up out of the land of Egypt, have acted perversely" (Exod. 32:7).

The scene between Moses and God resembles a mother who says to the dad after the misconduct of a child, *Your son needs to be punished.* In doing so she virtually relinquishes ownership and responsibility. God had every right to have had his fill of this obstinate people group. Note in Exodus 32:7 God's use of "you" and "your" that emphasizes Moses' role.

God gave Moses quite a challenge at this point. He expressed his extreme wrath, hot enough to consume the people. Further, he said in effect, *Don't bother intervening on their behalf. Let me alone. I've had it!* God offered to Moses to "make [of him] a great nation" (32:10). What a temptation that must have been to Moses. He and God had put up with so much from this rebellious people. Now God was offering to do away with them and make a great nation directly from Moses.

If we are honest, we will probably admit there have been times when we wished God would just get rid of those who hurt us so deeply. I wonder, though, if God made us that offer and said he would just be our God alone, could we do it? Remember God was dealing with a man of his own character, a man who had sold out his life to God. As Christians, we should fit that profile. Could we willingly take God away from those less deserving and never look back? Surely we could not. Neither could Moses.

Instead, Moses tossed responsibility for the people back to God. He asked, "O Lord, why does your wrath burn hot against *your* people?" (32:11, italics added for emphasis). Keep in mind, this question came before Moses actually saw what the people did. He could not imagine how God could be so angry. But we will witness his own intense anger when he first laid eyes on the desecration at the foot of the mountain.

Moses first appealed to God based on his own love for God and his desire to protect God's name. He knew what the charges would be: God had delivered his people only to destroy them. The pharaoh's lack of respect would appear justified and God's name would be in vain. Second, Moses reminded God of his promise to Abraham, Isaac, and Israel to multiply their descendants and to give the Promised Land to them to inherit forever. Moses claimed God could not renege on his promise.

God changed his mind. Notice Moses did not change God's mind. Although Moses interceded for the people, God was not having a weak moment of anger. His anger was righteous and just. In several instances, the word *relented* is used instead of *repented* (2 Samuel 24:16). The same concept can be found in Jonah 3:10, "When God saw what they did, how they turned from their evil ways, God changed his mind about the calamity that he had said he would bring upon them; and he did not do it." God was moved to pity and had compassion. God always leans toward mercy for his children. Once again, he offered the Israelites another chance.

Moses with the People (32:15–30)

When Moses reached the bottom of the mountain, his own anger flared. So angry was he that he dashed the cherished tablets on which God had just written the commandments. Confronting his brother, he received a reply limp enough to insult his intelligence: "I threw it [the gold jewelry] into the fire, and out came this calf!" (Exod. 32:24). Such an answer revealed a cowardly side of an otherwise good man. There seemed to be no reasonable explanation for this great apostasy. Turning one's back on God will never have an acceptable explanation.

Confronting a wrong or a sin is one step toward forgiving it. Moses confronted the people: "You have sinned a great sin" (32:30). They had to know the enormity of their sinful actions. But then Moses gave awesome words of hope: "Perhaps I can make atonement for your sin" (32:30).

Moses Before God (32:31–34)

That Moses would try to make atonement for the people is evidence of his character. Moses had always identified with the people. Even as a young man he had refused to be called the son of Pharaoh's daughter, and chose instead to "share ill treatment with the people of God" (Hebrews 11:24–25). One must wonder whether he realized how much ill treatment he would receive from the people of God. Even now, he was offering to give up his place in "the book" for the people. His dedication to them regardless of their treatment of him was remarkable.

Unlike the "book of life" referred to in the New Testament (Revelation 13:8; 17:8), the book Moses referred to is probably a record kept by God of those who are part of his people. "In the Old Testament this may simply mean people not in the book die, leaving the list of the living."[2] Consider Psalm 69:28, "Let them be blotted out of the book of the living." Whatever the book, Moses was choosing solidarity with the people, claiming to be a sinner, and asking God to take his life rather than theirs.

God refused to grant Moses his request and answered, "Whoever has sinned against me I will blot out of my book" (Exod. 32:33). These words were an Old Testament precursor to the priesthood of the believer. Each person would be responsible for his or her own relationship with God. Moses could not be the sacrifice for the Israelite people. That honor would go to Jesus Christ in God's perfect timing. Until then, continue on, God told Moses, "My angel shall go in front of you" (32:34).

For Life Today

Mrs. Dais's words were prophetic. Frank read the Gospels over and over and gave his life to Christ. Seventeen years later he was released on early parole. He had always identified with the inmates as his people, and he never turned his back on them after his release. He, his wife Ruth, and Mrs. Dais visited prisons across the nation for many years, sharing God's hope for inmates. Frank and Mrs. Dais are both now deceased, and Ruth carries on the prison ministry.

We have choices to make when people wrong us. We can turn away from them or turn to God on their behalf. Both Moses and Mrs. Dais approached God on behalf of others. Frank would intercede for prisoners for years. None of them glossed over the sins of the people but confronted them instead. And none of them deserted their people. Instead, they walked on with them. And God led the way.

Old Testament Heroes of the Faith

Many of the heroes of Old Testament faith emphasized intercessory prayer.

- Abraham interceded on behalf of his nephew Lot not to destroy Sodom (Genesis 18:23–25); he interceded for Abimelech, asking for healing (Gen. 20:17).
- Moses interceded for the Israelites after they built the golden calf (Exod. 32:11–14, 30–34).
- Samuel interceded for the people for forgiveness of idolatry (1 Sam. 7:5).

- David interceded all night on behalf of his newborn baby (2 Sam. 12:14–18); he interceded for the people when they took a census without God's direction (2 Sam. 24:17).
- Solomon interceded for the sinful people, asking for forgiveness (1 Kings 8).
- Elijah interceded for the widow that her child would live again (1 Kings 17:20–23).
- Hezekiah prayed for deliverance from the Assyrians (Isaiah 37:14–20).
- Amos prayed that God's word would not come to pass (Amos 7:5–6).
- Jeremiah pleaded for God not to be a stranger to whose who could not save themselves (Jeremiah 14:7–9).[3]

WHAT CAN WE LEARN FROM MOSES' EXPERIENCE?

- We must first spend time in the presence of God before we can intercede for others.
- We seek God's intervention first to witness to his glory.
- We persist with God on behalf of others, trusting his grace and mercy.

- We put our own interest behind us on behalf of those for whom we intercede.
- We do not deny our own emotional response to the wrongs of others.
- We have the courage to confront the wrongdoer with his or her actions.
- We offer to be used by God in his answer.
- We follow and obey whatever God's answer may be.

QUESTIONS

1. Would you classify the Israelites as Moses' friends? Why or why not?

2. Read Psalm 106:21–23. Moses stood in the breach between the people and God, and God did not destroy them. Did Moses take a risk with his intervention? If so, what was it?

LESSON 2: *Moses*

3. After Moses intervened for the Israelites with God, he still had to go back to the people. He confronted them with their sin. Does praying for someone substitute for holding him or her accountable for their wrong? Why or why not?

4. Read Jonah 3:9—4:5. What was the difference between Jonah's and Moses' reaction to God's change of mind?

5. Read Acts 7:60 and Romans 9:3. Stephen and Paul each offered their lives for those much less deserving. Have you been willing to sacrifice your all for someone to receive salvation? Reflect on what that would look like in a current relationship you have.

NOTES

1. Account based on the writer's personal knowledge.
2. Trent C. Butler, *Holman Bible Dictionary* (Nashville, TN: Holman Bible Publishers, 1991), see "book of life."
3. *Holman Bible Dictionary*, see "intercession."

FOCAL TEXT
Numbers 13:25—14:10a

BACKGROUND
Numbers 13—14;
Joshua 14:1–15

LESSON THREE

Caleb:
Showing Courageous Faith

MAIN IDEA

Caleb stood firmly for God's way even though his stand put him in conflict with most of the people.

QUESTION TO EXPLORE

How is God calling you to respond to him with courageous faith?

STUDY AIM

To identify from Caleb's actions how I will respond to God with courageous faith

QUICK READ

God chose twelve spies to investigate the Promised Land, but only two of those spies, Joshua and Caleb, chose God's way.

Finally! After two years and two months of journeying across the desert, the Israelites had arrived at the border of the Promised Land. Before them lay the land of Canaan, which God had promised to them through their ancestor Abraham. Imagine their excitement as the promised day arrived. For two years they had faithfully followed Moses and trusted God as they had been led by a cloud by day and a pillar of fire by night. Now they could finally leave the wilderness and move into their homeland, put down roots, and begin to rebuild their lives.

One might wish that the above scenario had occurred, but unfortunately, it did not happen this way. Instead, within a few weeks of leaving Egypt and beginning the journey in the wilderness, the Hebrews had begun to complain against both Moses and God. Many times they had so angered God that he was ready to destroy them and begin a new nation through Moses. Each time Moses interceded for the people, and God changed his mind concerning punishment. And each time, God led them on toward the Promised Land.

We should not be surprised that having arrived at their destination, their collective attitude was one of distrust and suspicion. We see here God's mercy in the face of the people's distrust. Moses stated, "All of you came to me and said, 'Let us send men ahead of us to explore the land for us and bring back a report to us regarding the route by which we should go up and the cities we will come to'" (Deuteronomy 1:22). The people seemed to have forgotten who had given them the route for two years through the wilderness.

Visualize coming to your destination after two years of hard journeying. God had promised he would give you this land "flowing with milk and honey" (Numbers 13:27; 14:8) for you and your descendants to have forever. Then try to picture yourself wanting to check it out first to decide whether you really want to enter.

Perhaps you have come to this spot yourself. God has clearly revealed to you the next step in his will for your life, but you hesitate and assess what it will mean for you and your family. Or maybe he has called you to a future of fulltime service to him, and you spend months or years trying to convince both yourself and God that you aren't capable. How many ministers I have heard say, *I ran from God for years before I accepted his call. I wasted so much time!*

We can learn a hard lesson from the behavior of the Israelites. Caleb, however, shows us a different view, one that pleased God.

Numbers 13:25–33

25 At the end of forty days they returned from exploring the land. **26** They came back to Moses and Aaron and the whole Israelite community at Kadesh in the Desert of Paran. There they reported to them and to the whole assembly and showed them the fruit of the land. **27** They gave Moses this account: "We went into the land to which you sent us, and it does flow with milk and honey! Here is its fruit. **28** But the people who live there are powerful, and the cities are fortified and very large. We even saw descendants of Anak there. **29** The Amalekites live in the Negev; the Hittites, Jebusites and Amorites live in the hill country; and the Canaanites live near the sea and along the Jordan." **30** Then Caleb silenced the people before Moses and said, "We should go up and take possession of the land, for we can certainly do it." **31** But the men who had gone up with him said, "We can't attack those people; they are stronger than we are." **32** And they spread among the Israelites a bad report about the land they had explored. They said, "The land we explored devours those living in it. All the people we saw there are of great size. **33** We saw the Nephilim there (the descendants of Anak come from the Nephilim). We seemed like grasshoppers in our own eyes, and we looked the same to them."

Numbers 14:1–10a

1 That night all the people of the community raised their voices and wept aloud. **2** All the Israelites grumbled against Moses and Aaron, and the whole assembly said to them, "If only we had died in Egypt! Or in this desert! **3** Why is the Lord bringing us to this land only to let us fall by the sword?

Our wives and children will be taken as plunder. Wouldn't it be better for us to go back to Egypt?" **4** And they said to each other, "We should choose a leader and go back to Egypt." **5** Then Moses and Aaron fell facedown in front of the whole Israelite assembly gathered there. **6** Joshua son of Nun and Caleb son of Jephunneh, who were among those who had explored the land, tore their clothes **7** and said to the entire Israelite assembly, "The land we passed through and explored is exceedingly good. **8** If the Lord is pleased with us, he will lead us into that land, a land flowing with milk and honey, and will give it to us. **9** Only do not rebel against the Lord. And do not be afraid of the people of the land, because we will swallow them up. Their protection is gone, but the Lord is with us. Do not be afraid of them." **10** But the whole assembly talked about stoning them.

In the Company of Cowards (13:25–29)

The spies with such little courage and no faith, unfortunately, were leaders. Each one represented his ancestral tribe. These tribes, originally descended from Jacob whose name God changed to Israel, were the social and political units of the Hebrew nation.

We may wonder how these leaders felt about their assignment of spying out the land of Canaan. Were they afraid? Did they go in with false pride of having been chosen for such a mission? Did they go in with faith and then lose it when faced with such huge obstacles? Or had they already lost their faith through the struggles of the two-year journey?

Whatever their attitude on entering, they quickly forgot God's promise to give them this land. Suddenly, when faced with the challenges before them, they thought only of their own limited strength. The dictionary defines a coward as "a person without courage."[1] They *looked the gift horse in the mouth* and decided not to receive the gift.

From Caleb's Perspective (13:30–33)

Two spies had a faith that would not fail them when faced with fear. Caleb, son of Jephunneh, was a forty-year-old member of the tribe of Judah. He saw the beauty of the Promised Land God was giving his people. He was enthralled with the land flowing with milk and honey. He had been in slavery all his life. Never had he seen such beauty and freedom!

Of course, he saw the Anakim and the fortified cities with thirteen-foot-thick walls. He was smart enough to realize those giants could eat him for lunch! But Caleb knew who was giving his people this enchanted land. He knew they had nothing to fear. No one had promised there would not be battles and skirmishes to take the land, but God had promised to be with them and give them the prize, his Promised Land.

Little is known of Caleb before this point in his life. What we see at the threshold of this new adventure is his courage. Courage is defined as "the capacity to meet danger without giving way to fear."[2] One would think Caleb's courage was demonstrated primarily in his attitude toward the giants occupying the land. Obviously he had confidence God would use the Israelites to defeat them. His real courage, however, would be called on in standing up to his own people, who would become the real enemy.

Caleb's only ally among the spies was Joshua, and the two of them stood together as a minority against the majority of ten spies. The majority quickly grew as the people began to weep and wail. On the other hand, the minority grew to only four: Caleb, Joshua, Moses, and Aaron. But these four stood with God, and together they formed the real majority.

When It's Us Against Them (14:1–10a)

Once again, the people wept and complained against Moses and Aaron. Their lack of logic was almost comical. They asked why God would bring them this far to be killed in battle. Furthermore, their wives and children would become booty for the enemy. Their irrational thinking led to panic, and they decided to elect a new captain and go back to Egypt.

At this critical juncture, the Israelites chose to believe the ten spies with a negative report rather than the two with a positive report. Just given the numbers, such confidence may be logical. But when God has made a promise, statistics do not matter. Instead, the people let the threat of slavery, the wrath of the new Pharaoh, and fear for the lives of their newborn boys overrule their faith in God and his leaders.

Moses, Aaron, Caleb, and Joshua could see their dream of receiving God's promise falling apart. Still they appealed to the people with an outward sign of an inner grief by falling prostrate on their faces and tearing their clothes. Caleb and Joshua verbally implored the people to listen to the truth. If only they would halt this rebellion and turn toward God, the land would be theirs for the taking (Num. 14:9).

With mass panic, the people threatened to stone Caleb, Joshua, Moses, and Aaron. The people failed to recognize that, in doing so, they would cut off their communication with God. Without Moses their eyes would see, but their ears would not hear.

This battle of the wills was not about the land. Rather it was about faith. The difficulty they would face in taking the land was only a scapegoat for the fact that they had lost their faith in God. We have our scapegoats, too. They are more commonly called excuses. *As soon as the kids are out of college, Lord, we'll give up everything and move to the mission field. When I retire, Lord, I'll have time to*

LESSON 3: *Caleb*

help in the homeless mission. But God, I've never even been to college. You expect me to do what?

When God Has Had Enough (14:20–25)

Caleb's courage was about to be tested again. Although God determined not to strike the complaining people with pestilence and disinherit them (Num. 14:12), he consigned them to wander in the wilderness for forty years, one year for every day the spies were in the Promised Land. Caleb and Joshua, although they were ready to take the new land, would of necessity wander with them.

If we defy God's will for us, our actions will impact others. Our mates, our children, and others will usually have to go with us, forfeiting the blessing God had for them. They will suffer the consequences with us. But there will always be hope. God saw Caleb's courage and rewarded him. "But my servant Caleb, because he has a different spirit and has followed me wholeheartedly, I will bring into the land into which he went, and his descendants shall possess it" (14:24).

Forty years later, God kept his promise, and eighty-five-year-old Caleb entered the Promised Land along with Joshua, Moses' successor (14:7–10). They were rewarded for their faithfulness and courage. They had to wait for it. The people wandered aimlessly, but Caleb and Joshua were not wandering. Instead, they were journeying toward a promise. All men over the age of twenty would die in the wilderness, but Caleb and Joshua would live long lives serving God in the Promised Land.

For Life Today

Each of us will, at least one time in our lives, experience a Caleb-type opportunity. One of mine came several years ago in the form of an overseas mission trip. My lack of finances loomed as large as the Anakim giants. If that wasn't enough, I would be leaving my group in South Africa and flying alone into Zimbabwe, a country devastated through the governing of an evil dictator.

I had clearly heard God's call to make this trip. I knew he would provide financial help. He did. I knew he would protect me as I spent three days in a dangerous environment. He did. One of my vivid memories is standing on the twelfth floor of a downtown Harare hotel one night, looking down at the lights below. I cried out to God, "What am I doing here, God? What do you want me to do with this unbelievable opportunity?" God is continuing to answer that question, and I've since returned for a longer trip.

Your Caleb moment may come in the form of a ministry opportunity. It may be choosing your mate. Or, with the world growing smaller every day, your moment may look like mine—go into all the world. When the opportunity looks like the Promised Land, God will expect us to look like Caleb.

QUESTIONS

1. Who makes up a majority of influences in your life? Do they have a positive or a negative effect on your life? (Consider co-workers, church congregation, family, and others.)

2. The spies went into the Promised Land to make plans for strategic purposes. Instead they cut out their plans completely. They quit. Do you expect obstacles on your journey of faith? How do you respond to them?

3. Caleb, Numbers 14:24 states, was a man of a different spirit and followed God fully. What would that mean in your life today? Might you count the cost as too high? Or do you have a different spirit?

4. God rewarded Caleb for his courage forty-five years later. Meanwhile, he had to suffer with his people. How do you think you might have handled that forty-five-year wait? How do you handle waiting on God now? How does that wait require courage?

The Anakim

Who were these giants the spies found in the Promised Land? Their clan name, Anakim, meant *long-necked* or *strong-necked*. Anak was their ancestor. These giants were part of the Nephilim, a race of giants originating from when the sons of God went in to the daughters of humans, who bore children to them (Genesis 6:4).[3] They were the warriors of renown, and the spies' description of their intimidating warlike appearance filled the Israelites with terror.

One can see how the size and appearance of these warrior giants would terrorize former slaves who had just spent two years in the wilderness. In fact, the Philistine giants whom David encountered in 2 Samuel 21:15–22 were descendants of the Anakim.

After the Israelites entered Canaan, Joshua finally expelled them from the land. However, a remnant of them found refuge in the cities of Gaza, Gath, and Ashdod (Joshua 11:21–22). Descendants of these giants from Gath would later be killed in a battle between them and King David's men (1 Samuel 21:18–22).

CASE STUDY

Joey was a youth pastor in a church in the South. For months he had been restless, feeling God nudging him toward another ministry. He had no idea what it was. Joey heard a speaker from New York and suddenly knew his mission. There was strong need for youth ministry in a mission church in Harlem.

Joey and his wife visited Harlem. The crime rate in the neighborhood in which they would live and serve was so high people were moving out, not in. The city was huge. The thought of raising their children there petrified his wife. But Joey felt a challenge like never before. How should Joey and his wife proceed? What steps should they take?

NOTES

1. *The New Lexicon Webster's Dictionary of the English Language* (New York: Lexicon Publications, Inc., 1989), see "Coward."

2. *The New Lexicon Webster's Dictionary of the English Language*, see "Courage."

3. Trent C. Butler, General Editor, *Holman Bible Dictionary* (Nashville: Holman Bible Publishers, 1991), see "Anak, Anakim," "Nephilim."

FOCAL TEXT
Numbers 27:1–11

BACKGROUND
Numbers 27:1–11; 36:1–12

LESSON FOUR

The Sisterhood:
Challenging Unfairness

MAIN IDEA

The sisters challenged the unfair laws and customs that prevented women from inheriting land.

QUESTION TO EXPLORE

Should God's people care about discrimination?

STUDY AIM

To describe the sisters' challenge to the unfair laws and customs that prevented women from inheriting land and consider how this Scripture calls me to challenge unfair laws and customs

QUICK READ

Brave women, the daughters of Zelophehad, challenged an unfair law over inheritance rights and were victorious.

In 1829, in Charleston, South Carolina, Angelina Grimke, a twenty-four-year-old single woman, challenged church leadership to speak out against slavery. Rather than consider her challenge, the church promptly expelled her. Being the Southern lady she was, she decided to leave Charleston rather than cause more conflict. Her sister Sarah, of like mind on this issue, was an abolitionist speaker in the North. Where better could Angelina go to continue her challenge to slavery? She said in one speech: "I know you [women] do not make the laws, but I know that you are the wives and mothers, the sisters and daughters of those who do; and if you really suppose that we can do nothing to overthrow slavery you are greatly mistaken.... Let your sentiments be known."[1]

Nine years after confronting church leadership, Angelina found herself standing in front of a legislative body in a crowded Massachusetts statehouse and stating:

> I stand before you as a repentant slave owner....
> I feel that I owe it to the suffering slave and to the deluded master, to my country and to the world, to do all I can to overturn a system of complicated crimes, built upon the broken hearts and prostrate bodies of my countrymen in chains and cemented by the blood, sweat and tears of my sisters in chains.[2]

Sarah Grimke, Angelina's older sister, authored *Epistle to the Clergy of the Southern States*, identifying Scripture from the Old and New Testaments to declare that the Bible could not be used to justify slavery. Together, the sisters produced a documentation of slavery, *American Slavery As It Is*, which became a bestseller in England and America and greatly influenced Harriet Beecher Stowe's *Uncle Tom's Cabin*. Sarah wrote *Letters on the Equality of the Sexes and the Condition of Women*, published in 1838.

These two sisters, Sarah and Angelina Grimke, were not instantly successful when they tackled slavery, but they made great strides toward its eventual overturn. Centuries before, the five daughters of Zelophehad also challenged an unfair law.

Numbers 27:1–11

[1] The daughters of Zelophehad son of Hepher, the son of Gilead, the son of Makir, the son of Manasseh, belonged to the clans of Manasseh son of Joseph. The names of the daughters were Mahlah, Noah, Hoglah, Milcah and Tirzah. They approached [2] the entrance to the Tent of Meeting and stood before Moses, Eleazar the priest, the leaders and the whole assembly, and said, [3] "Our father died in the desert. He was not among Korah's followers, who banded together

against the LORD, but he died for his own sin and left no sons. **4** Why should our father's name disappear from his clan because he had no son? Give us property among our father's relatives." **5** So Moses brought their case before the LORD **6** and the LORD said to him, **7** "What Zelophehad's daughters are saying is right. You must certainly give them property as an inheritance among their father's relatives and turn their father's inheritance over to them. **8** "Say to the Israelites, 'If a man dies and leaves no son, turn his inheritance over to his daughter. **9** If he has no daughter, give his inheritance to his brothers. **10** If he has no brothers, give his inheritance to his father's brothers. **11** If his father had no brothers, give his inheritance to the nearest relative in his clan, that he may possess it. This is to be a legal requirement for the Israelites, as the LORD commanded Moses.'"

Who Are the Daughters of Zelophehad? (27:1)

The background Scripture of the previous lesson stated that God had sworn to the people that no one who was over twenty would live to see the Promised Land, except Caleb and Joshua (see Numbers 14:20–23, 28–29). Due to the rebellion of the Israelites at Kadesh-barnea, everyone who was in the generation that had been delivered from Egypt would die. Zelophehad, of the tribe of Manasseh, was one of those who died. His daughters said he died for his own sin. He may have committed a personal sin for which he was punished by death.

Regardless of how Zelophehad died, he died without any sons as heirs. However, he had five daughters. Most women in the Bible were not identified by name. Zelophehad's daughters, Mahlah, Noah, Hoglah, Milcah, and Tirzah, are five of the only 170 named women in the Bible.[3] We may assume their mother was not living and they were their father's sole heirs. Interestingly, at least three of the daughters' names coincide with the names of towns west of the Jordan: Noah in Zebulun (Joshua 19:13), Hoglah in Judah (Josh. 15:6), and Tirzah in Manasseh (Josh. 12:24; 1 Kings 15:21). The Promised Land was west of the Jordan, and so Zelophehad and his wife may have named their daughters accordingly as a sign of faith. As is common with Hebrew names, each of their names had meaning. Mahlah means *weak* or *sickly*. Noah means *rest* or *comfort*. Hoglah means *partridge;* Milcah, *counselor*. The meaning of Tirzah is unknown.[4]

Their ages also are unknown. More than likely they were children of the wilderness, born and reared there. Whatever their ages, they were intelligent and bold young women. They knew the law. They understood what was about to happen to their father's portion of land. They also had the courage to take their case to Moses. For women, this privilege was virtually unheard of.

What Was Their Case? (27:2–4)

At first glance, the problem the sisters brought before Moses appeared to be solely about inheritance laws. But, as we shall see, it had far-reaching ramifications. The laws concerning inheritances were male-dominated. After all, the culture was so patriarchal that women did not even count in the census. In a sense these women were literally *no-count* girls daring to come before the holy man of God. And God heard them. What encouragement! No matter what our status in life, when we bring our problems to God, God listens.

Women could not legally own land at the time the Israelites were possessing the Promised Land. All land was passed through the male members of the family. If a man died and had no sons, his inheritance would pass to his brothers. If he had no brothers, it would go to his father's brothers. Finally, if there were no brothers or uncles, it would go to his next male kinsman. One thing was for sure. The land would definitely not go to his daughters.

The daughters used an argument based on respect for their father. Why, they asked, should their father's death cause his name to be taken away from his Manasseh clan? If this happened, when the time came for the Promised Land to be parceled out among the tribes, the Manasseh clan would be shortchanged (Num. 26:54–56). Their father's name would be forgotten, and they would be the end of his line without any property or heirs. This law, they argued, was unfair.

What Was the Verdict? (27:5–11)

Moses must have listened to thousands of disputes among families over the years he had been leading Israel. At one point his father-in-law, Jethro, told him he was hearing too many. Jethro advised Moses to accept only the hard cases and appoint judges to handle the minor disputes. The major cases Moses would take to God (see Exodus 18:17–27). Because these women had such a valid argument, they took their case to Moses, and he took it directly to God.

God decided in the daughters' favor. Not only were they granted the inheritance they asked for, but God also gave all Israel a new law. The language in Numbers 27:8 was directed to the general public. All would be liable to this law. This new law simply inserted one step into the old way of passing down land. But what a major step it was! The land would first be given to a man's daughters upon his death if he had no sons. If there were no children at all, then the original line of inheritance would continue with his brothers.

Why Did It Matter to the Israelites? (Numbers 36)

To the minds of the Israelite tribal leaders, this original law of inheritance existed for a reason. They did not see it as only a matter of women's rights. In Numbers 36, the heads of the ancestral houses of the Manasseh clan approached Moses and all other heads of ancestral houses. They saw this as a far-reaching problem affecting not only their tribe in the future but also others.

This was the problem: if these daughters, and all others following them, married outside their tribe, their inheritance would be added to the tribe into which they married. Their father's tribe would lose their allotted portion of land. Further, when the Israelite Year of Jubilee came, the land would be inherited by the new tribe to be passed down in their line forever.[5] In other words, Manasseh's tribe would never get it back. Land was their economy in that day, and Manasseh's tribe would suffer.

Moses agreed with the tribal leaders. God showed him they were right. To remedy this possibility, the daughters of Zelophehad and all other daughters who would possess an inheritance must marry into a clan of their father's tribe. Interestingly, God added that other than these boundaries, the women could marry whomever they chose. In this way, all Israelites would continue to possess their ancestral inheritance, and no lands would be so transferred from tribe to tribe. The daughters of Zelophehad did just that. All five of them married their cousins.

When the land allotments were actually made, these daughters appeared one more time before the priests and leaders (Num. 17:3–6). They approached the priest Eleazar, and Joshua, successor to Moses, and other leaders. As a reminder, they told the leaders God had commanded

Moses to give them an inheritance along with their male kin. That day ten portions were added to Manasseh's allotment. According to custom, each daughter received a double portion because their father Zelophehad was the firstborn son. Thus the five daughters of Zelophehad challenged an unfair law, saved their father's honor, added land to the Manasseh tribe, and facilitated a new law that would serve women in the future.

What Does This Mean Today?

Women's rights are certainly not the only hot topic in today's culture that reveals unfair laws. Immigration, human trafficking, and other global problems shed light on laws that stunt any possible healing or release of oppression. Many victims, children and adults, suffer and die every day because of unfair laws. For others the results are not death but a life of subjection, poverty, sickness, and despair.

As Christians, we cannot deny our responsibility for bringing good news to the poor, proclaiming release to the captives, recovering sight for the blind, and bringing freedom to the oppressed (Luke 4:18). We can learn much from these brave women. They stood up for their rights. In so doing, they stood up for the inheritance rights of women for generations to come.

We will most likely be able to make the greatest changes in the areas about which we are passionate. Look around.

It won't take long to see even subtle wrongs in our society. Ask God how he can use you. Then ask him to ignite a passion in you that will not cease until you have taken action toward fairness. We will not change the world alone, but each of us can take a first step.

Biblical Precedent

This case is believed today to be one of the earliest reported lawsuits on record. An American Bar Association Journal article in February, 1924, quotes this decision in favor of the daughters of Zelophehad. The author described it as an "early declaratory judgment in which the property rights of women marrying outside of their tribe are clearly set forth."[6] This case was not only a victory for those who filed it but also for women for centuries to come.

The Year of Jubilee (Leviticus 25)

Every fiftieth year, after seven cycles of seven years, came a Year of Jubilee. Three things were to happen in this year. (1) The soil of the fields was to rest; there should be no tending or planting. God said he would bring a blessing on crops of the sixth year so they would bring a harvest for three years. (2) All land was to revert to its original owner. The original distribution of land was to remain intact. (3) All slaves were to be set free. The Year of Jubilee had a leveling effect on Israel's culture. It discouraged obsessive accumulation of wealth. It assured that no Israelite would be deprived of his inheritance. Most importantly, the year was a constant reminder of God's interest in economic justice.[7]

Although this practice has long since been foregone, what would be the effect on our world if it or its principles were implemented today? What would it look like if we had a *what-is-mine-is-yours* attitude, realizing that everything belongs to God? We are only stewards without true ownership of anything.

How to Fight Unfairness

Unfairness may exist in families, churches, and communities as well as in larger domains. We can learn from these five sisters how to fight unfairness.

- They did not grumble among the people about the unfairness of the law.
- They did not act like victims.
- They took their concerns to the proper authorities.
- They respectfully presented their case.
- They waited for the verdict.

- They followed up to make sure the verdict was carried out.

Even though we may not always receive the verdict we desire, such an approach will allow us to be taken seriously.

QUESTIONS

1. Would you say these sisters were militant in their approach to their request?

2. Were they doormats to be walked on? What are some of the qualities you see in them that most likely gained them an audience with Moses?

3. Have you been challenged with an unfair law that affected you or someone you love? What was your response at the time? Would it be any different now?

4. Does anger serve us well when faced with unfairness? What is the difference in righteous anger and selfish anger? If anger fuels your passion, how can you refuel?

5. What was the importance of the sisters showing up at allotment time to make sure they received their inheritance? Why is follow-up so important in an effort to change the system?

NOTES

1. Harold Ivan Smith, *A Singular Devotion* (New Jersey: Fleming H. Revel Company, 1990), 53.
2. Smith, 53–54.
3. Lisa Wilson Davidson, *Preaching the Women of the Bible* (St. Louis: Chalice Press, 2006), 35.
4. Sue Poorman Richards and Lawrence O. Richards, *Women of the Bible* (Nashville: Thomas Nelson, 2003), 255.
5. See Leviticus 25; Deuteronomy 15; and the small article, "The Year of Jubilee (Leviticus 25)."
6. Edith Deen, *All the Women of the Bible* (Edison, NJ: Castle Books, 1955), 63.
7. Trent C. Butler, General Editor, *Holman Bible Dictionary* (Nashville: Holman Bible Publishers, 1991), see "Year of Jubilee."

FOCAL TEXT
Joshua 24:1–3, 13–27

BACKGROUND
Joshua 24

LESSON FIVE

Joshua:
Leading in Following God

MAIN IDEA

Joshua led his people to follow God faithfully.

QUESTION TO EXPLORE

How are you leading others to follow God faithfully?

STUDY AIM

To commit myself definitely and fully to follow God and lead others to do so

QUICK READ

After leading them in battle for twenty years, Joshua led the people to recommit themselves to the covenant and to following God.

To desire to live a life of purpose and meaning is a characteristic of most if not all people, although they may define it differently. We are willing to follow almost anyone or anything that appears to offer the path to that end. For most of us, while we were children, our parents served as our primary guides on this journey. But once we left home, we were forced to find our own path. What we quickly discovered was that there is a myriad of competing voices, all wrapped in appealing packaging and reasonable arguments crying, *follow me to happiness and fulfillment.* All too often, however, as we followed those voices, we found the offer was empty and our longing for meaning even deeper.

For forty years, the Israelites had followed Moses through the desert, and for twenty years, they had followed Joshua as he led them in conquest of the Promised Land. Then came the time for them to settle in their new homes and fulfill the promise of blessing God had made to their ancestor Abraham. But they would do so without a single unifying leader and would be forced to choose whether to follow God or the gods of the other nations. Joshua here reminded them they were called to follow God and to lead others to follow God also. As believers, we carry that same call—to follow God's path through a world full of alternative paths by maintaining a consistent commitment and to lead others in doing so as well.

LESSON 5: *Joshua*

JOSHUA 24:1–3, 13–27

1 Then Joshua gathered all the tribes of Israel to Shechem, and called for the elders of Israel and for their heads and their judges and their officers; and they presented themselves before God. **2** Joshua said to all the people, "Thus says the LORD, the God of Israel, 'From ancient times your fathers lived beyond the River, namely, Terah, the father of Abraham and the father of Nahor, and they served other gods. **3** 'Then I took your father Abraham from beyond the River, and led him through all the land of Canaan, and multiplied his descendants and gave him Isaac.

• • • • • • • • • • • • • • • • • • • •

13 'I gave you a land on which you had not labored, and cities which you had not built, and you have lived in them; you are eating of vineyards and olive groves which you did not plant.' **14** "Now, therefore, fear the LORD and serve Him in sincerity and truth; and put away the gods which your fathers served beyond the River and in Egypt, and serve the LORD. **15** "If it is disagreeable in your sight to serve the LORD, choose for yourselves today whom you will serve: whether the gods which your fathers served which were beyond the River, or the gods of the Amorites in whose land you are living; but as for me and my house, we will serve the LORD." **16** The people answered and said, "Far be it from us that we should forsake the LORD to serve other gods; **17** for the LORD our God is He who brought us and our fathers up out of the land of Egypt, from the house of bondage, and who did these great signs in our sight and preserved us through all the way in which we went and among all the peoples through whose midst we passed. **18** "The Lord drove out from before us all the peoples, even the Amorites who lived in the land. We also will serve the Lord, for He is our God." **19** Then Joshua said to the people, "You will not be able to serve the Lord, for He is a holy God. He is a jealous God; He will not forgive your transgression or your sins. **20** "If you forsake the Lord and serve foreign gods, then He will turn and do you harm and consume you after He has done good to you." **21** The people said to Joshua, "No, but we will serve the Lord." **22** Joshua said to the people, "You are witnesses against yourselves that you have chosen for yourselves the Lord, to serve Him." And they said, "We are witnesses." **23** "Now therefore, put away the foreign gods which are in your midst, and incline your hearts to the Lord, the God of Israel." **24** The people said to Joshua, "We will serve the Lord our God and we will obey His voice." **25** So Joshua made a covenant with the people that day, and made for them a statute and an ordinance in Shechem. **26** And Joshua wrote these words in the book of the law of God; and he took a large stone and set it up there under the oak that was by the sanctuary of the Lord. **27** Joshua said to all the people, "Behold, this stone shall be for a witness against us, for it has heard all the words of the Lord which He spoke to us; thus it shall be for a witness against you, so that you do not deny your God."

The Urgent Call (24:1–3a, 13–15)

After Joshua had gathered the people together, he reminded them of where they came from. He reminded them God had called their ancestor Abraham to leave his homeland "beyond the River" and promised to Abraham's descendants this land.[1] The phrase "beyond the River" refers to the great river Euphrates, which ran through the land of Babylon. Abraham's family was from "Ur of the Chaldeans" which was located in Mesopotamia (Genesis 11:31–32). This, the land of the Babylonians, is modern Iraq.

Joshua's statement that Abraham's family "served other gods" might surprise some. These words reminded the hearers that Abraham had grown up with the polytheistic beliefs of Mesopotamia. God had called Abraham out of worshiping various gods to the worship of the one true God.

Joshua then summarized the history of the Israelite people from Abraham until the current generation before him (Joshua 24:4–13). The main thing to notice in these verses is that, even though this is the history of the Israelite people, the subject of every sentence is God. Joshua used the first person pronoun to make it clear God had fulfilled the promise of many descendants. God had brought the plagues on Egypt and liberated the Israelites from slavery. God had led and sustained them as they crossed the desert wilderness. And God had driven the inhabitants of Canaan out of the land before the Israelites. God had now given them a fertile land with crops they had not planted and houses they had not built. The purpose of retelling this history was to remind the people that it was God and not the gods their ancestors had worshiped in Babylon who had acted on their behalf.

In verses 14–15, Joshua came to his point by clearly calling the people to make a choice. They must choose whether they would follow and worship God or the gods of Babylon and Egypt. This reference seems to indicate that the people had worshiped the gods of Egypt during their time there. Because the people came from a long tradition of worshiping many gods, they perhaps saw no problem with worshiping both God and the other gods. For many years, the people had been under the leadership of Moses and Joshua, who had sought through words and actions to lead them to follow only God. Now Joshua knew those days were ending, and it would be up to the people to choose for themselves. So he clearly stated that a choice must be made. He was not suggesting that the choice to worship the false gods would be acceptable. He was calling for a choice and encouraging them to choose to follow God. He concluded by stating that whatever the rest of the people might choose, he and his household would continue to serve God.

The Initial Commitment (24:16–18)

The people answered Joshua's call together. They agreed that God had been good to them and recalled how God had delivered them from slavery in Egypt. They remembered how he had protected them on their journey to the Promised Land and recognized that it was God who had defeated all their enemies. With one voice they declared they too would be obedient and serve God. It is important to notice that the response of the people was clearly based on their recognition that God had greatly blessed them in the past.

Throughout the Ancient Near East, the worship of the false gods was based on fear of what the gods might do if the people stopped offering their sacrifices. There was no sense in which the gods acted on behalf of the people. There was certainly no idea that a god or gods would enter into a covenant relationship with humans. The gods were seen as highly capricious and selfish, and humanity was simply the slaves of the gods. The God of Israel, though, loved humanity and was constantly seeking to draw humanity into a relationship not as slaves, but as children. The people's statement indicates that their commitment was not made from fear of God's capricious wrath, but from gratitude for what God had already done for them.

The Clear Warning (24:19–20)

Joshua's response in verse 19 might surprise some readers. He told them they would be unable to serve God. Why would he say this? Joshua understood something about human nature, and he specifically knew this people. He knew that, as they stood there that day, the people could easily say they would follow. But once they were away from his leadership and on their own, it would be just as easy to turn to the false gods they had known before.

Today we share the same human nature as the Israelites. It is often easy to commit to following God when we are surrounded by other believers in a time of worship. But once we leave and are alone, it can be easy to fall into old habits. Joshua did not want them to think all they had to do was promise to follow God. He reminded them if they did not keep this promise, God would punish them. Joshua wanted them to consider that the commitment they were making would be difficult to keep when they left to go to their new homes. He let them know God is a holy and jealous God who does not take it lightly when his people turn away and serve other gods. Although the people were in a covenant with God, God would not be bound to continue to bless them if the people broke the covenant by violating God's requirement of exclusive devotion.

The Renewed Covenant (24:21–27)

The people cried out in protest that they would surely keep their promise to serve God alone. Their words seemed to indicate they understood this commitment was not made lightly and would require constant attention to keep.

Once again Joshua challenged their statement and ability to keep the commitment. This time he pointed out that their statement would serve as witness against them should they ever break their promise.

Some may question whether Joshua was being too harsh with the people by not accepting their words. But his actions merely indicated the absolute seriousness of this commitment. He wanted the people to clearly understand this was a solemn personal promise for which God would hold them accountable. They could not blame Joshua or anyone else if they failed to follow through. Having made this commitment, any violation would be a negative reflection on God. As God's people they bore God's name, and any action that violated God's covenant would do damage to that name and they would incur God's judgment. Perhaps today, some believers take their initial commitment lightly. Perhaps those of us who live where being a Christian is somewhat easy have lost some of the seriousness of bearing that name.

Once the people had promised to worship God, Joshua called for action. He told them to throw away their idols because these idols would take their attention and devotion away from God.

After the people agreed, Joshua made a new covenant with the people. This covenant was not really new but was the same covenant Moses had led the people to make with

God at Mount Sinai. This covenant put in writing the people's promise to follow and obey God and reminded the people of what God expected.

Joshua was careful to write down the words of this covenant for future generations. Verse 26 states that Joshua set up a stone near the sanctuary as a memorial. Such memorial stones were often quite large and were commonly used as permanent reminders of significant events. Often Egyptian and Mesopotamian kings would set up stones at the site of great victories and engrave them with accounts of the battle. In the Old Testament, people often set up stone monuments without engraving at places where they had encountered God or where God had intervened on their behalf (see Gen. 28:18; 35:14; 1 Samuel 7:12). Here the stone would be more than a reminder of their commitment; it would be a witness and evidence against them should they break that commitment. It would also serve as a teaching aid as they sought to lead future generations to follow God.

Implications for Today

In our world, many things call to us claiming to be the path to happiness. The Bible clearly teaches us that the only path that will truly lead to fulfillment in life is to follow God through surrender to Jesus.

The decision to follow God is the single most important decision a person will ever make and should not be taken lightly. The choice to follow God means that we refuse to follow any other path. We cannot faithfully serve God if we are focused on pursuing the things of this world. For those of us who have followed God's path, we know the peace, joy, and hope it brings. Our duty then is to help others discover all God has for them when they commit to follow him.

Leading Someone to Follow God

By examining the life of Joshua, we can see that in order to be able to lead someone in following God, we should

- Consistently live our personal commitment to God
- Remind the other person of God's faithfulness and actions
- Call for a specific verbal commitment to follow
- Write down or set up some form of memorial of the commitment as a reminder
- Be available to encourage and support as the other person follows

Shechem

The city of Shechem was an ideal place at which to hold a significant covenant renewal ceremony. Archaeological evidence suggests that Shechem was one of the oldest and most significant cultural urban centers in Canaan prior to the arrival of the Israelites. Shechem was the first place Abram stopped after he left his father's home, and it was where God had stated the promise to give the land to Abram's descendants (Gen. 12:6–7). Shechem was also where Jacob had purchased a plot of land and erected an altar to God after his reunion with Esau (Gen. 33:18–20). Shechem is located between Mount Ebal and Mount Gerizim, where the people had first reaffirmed their covenant after the defeat of Ai as Moses had commanded (Josh. 8:30–35). Due to these associations, this city maintained an important place in Israel until the Assryians destroyed the city in 722 B.C. during their conquest of the Northern Kingdom.

QUESTIONS

1. Have you ever had an experience of leading someone in trusting God through a time of decision? What happened?

LESSON 5: *Joshua*

2. What events in your life do you remember as times when God most clearly helped you?

3. What part of this lesson has been most challenging to you? Why?

4. How can you tell when someone is fully trusting and following God?

NOTES

1. Unless otherwise indicated, all Scripture quotations in lessons 5–8 are from the New American Standard Bible.

FOCAL TEXT
Judges 4:1–16; 5:1–7

BACKGROUND
Judges 4—5

LESSON SIX

Deborah:
Exercising Strong Leadership

MAIN IDEA

Deborah, a prophetess and judge, delivered God's message to Barak and exercised strong leadership in defeating Israel's enemies.

QUESTION TO EXPLORE

How can women serve God?

STUDY AIM

To consider the meaning for today of Deborah's role in serving God and bringing deliverance to Israel

QUICK READ

God told the prophetess Deborah to tell Barak to lead the army against the Canaanites. When Barak refused to lead without Deborah's help, Deborah led the Israelites in defeating their enemies.

Take just a minute and think back over your life. Apart from your parents, who first taught you about God? Who first told you the stories from the Bible? For many, it was a female Sunday School teacher. Some of God's best leaders have been women. There are many examples of this in the Bible. In the Old Testament, Miriam was a prophetess and leader of the Israelites (Exodus 15:20; Micah 6:4). Esther helped save the Israelites (see lesson fourteen). In the New Testament, Paul named women who were leaders in the church: Phoebe, Priscilla, and Junia. Many other great women have faithfully served as leaders throughout the history of the church. God has given women, like all believers, special gifts and wants women to be able to use those gifts in the church.

Judges 4—5 tells a story about two very different women. Deborah was one of the greatest female leaders in the Bible. She was a prophetess and judge who spoke God's message to the Israelites and led them to defeat their enemy. The other woman, Jael, was not wealthy and was not a leader of the people. In fact, she was not even an Israelite. Yet she played an important role in God's plan to save his people. Through this story, we can learn that it does not matter to God whether you are a man or a woman or you are rich or poor. If we trust God, God will help us to exercise leadership in fulfilling his plans.

LESSON 6: *Deborah*

JUDGES 4:1–16

1 Then the sons of Israel again did evil in the sight of the LORD, after Ehud died. **2** And the LORD sold them into the hand of Jabin king of Canaan, who reigned in Hazor; and the commander of his army was Sisera, who lived in Harosheth-hagoyim. **3** The sons of Israel cried to the LORD; for he had nine hundred iron chariots, and he oppressed the sons of Israel severely for twenty years. **4** Now Deborah, a prophetess, the wife of Lappidoth, was judging Israel at that time. **5** She used to sit under the palm tree of Deborah between Ramah and Bethel in the hill country of Ephraim; and the sons of Israel came up to her for judgment. **6** Now she sent and summoned Barak the son of Abinoam from Kedesh-naphtali, and said to him, "Behold, the LORD, the God of Israel, has commanded, 'Go and march to Mount Tabor, and take with you ten thousand men from the sons of Naphtali and from the sons of Zebulun. **7** 'I will draw out to you Sisera, the commander of Jabin's army, with his chariots and his many troops to the river Kishon, and I will give him into your hand.'" **8** Then Barak said to her, "If you will go with me, then I will go; but if you will not go with me, I will not go." **9** She said, "I will surely go with you; nevertheless, the honor shall not be yours on the journey that you are about to take, for the LORD will sell Sisera into the hands of a woman." Then Deborah arose and went with Barak to Kedesh. **10** Barak called Zebulun and Naphtali together to Kedesh, and ten thousand men went up with him; Deborah also went up with him. **11** Now Heber the Kenite had separated himself from the Kenites, from the sons of Hobab the father-in-law of Moses, and had pitched his tent as far away as the oak in Zaanannim, which is near Kedesh. **12** Then they told Sisera that Barak the son of Abinoam had gone up to Mount Tabor. **13** Sisera called together all his chariots, nine hundred iron chariots, and all the people who were with him, from Harosheth-hagoyim to the river Kishon. **14** Deborah said to Barak, "Arise! For this is the day in which the Lord has given Sisera into your hands; behold, the Lord has gone out before you." So Barak went down from Mount Tabor with ten thousand men following him. **15** The Lord routed Sisera and all his chariots and all his army with the edge of the sword before Barak; and Sisera alighted from his chariot and fled away on foot. **16** But Barak pursued the chariots and the army as far as Harosheth-hagoyim, and all the army of Sisera fell by the edge of the sword; not even one was left.

Judges 5:1–7

1 Then Deborah and Barak the son of Abinoam sang on that day, saying,
  2 "That the leaders led in Israel,
    That the people volunteered,
    Bless the Lord!

3 "Hear, O kings; give ear, O rulers!
  I—to the Lord, I will sing,
  I will sing praise to the Lord, the God of Israel.
4 "Lord, when You went out from Seir,
  When You marched from the field of Edom,
  The earth quaked, the heavens also dripped,
  Even the clouds dripped water.
5 "The mountains quaked at the presence of the Lord,
  This Sinai, at the presence of the Lord, the God of Israel.
6 "In the days of Shamgar the son of Anath,
  In the days of Jael, the highways were deserted,
  And travelers went by roundabout ways.
7 "The peasantry ceased, they ceased in Israel,
  Until I, Deborah, arose,
  Until I arose, a mother in Israel.

God Punishes Israel (4:1–3)

After Joshua died, the Israelites continued to fight against their enemies so that they could settle in the Promised Land. Judges 2:11–19 describes a repeating pattern of sin, judgment, and deliverance. As the people were exposed to the pagan worship of the Canaanites, they began to follow and worship the false gods. The worship of these false gods offered the people something they found attractive, and many may not have seen any harm in worshiping both

God and the pagan gods. Yet God had told them they were to worship God alone, and so God punished them by sending an enemy to rule over and oppress them. When the people cried out to God for help, God sent a judge to free them and lead them back to God. Once that judge died, the people returned to their sin and the cycle repeated.

Ehud, one of the first judges, rescued the Israelites from the Moabites and brought peace to Israel for eighty years. Yet after he died, the people once again started to worship the false gods of the Canaanites. God became angry with the people and sent Jabin, the king of Hazor, to rule over the Israelites.

Jabin had a large army that included 900 chariots made of iron in addition to a large number of foot soldiers. The number of chariots required a large number of horses as well as highly trained drivers and mounted archers. The nature of this army indicates that Jabin and his general Sisera depended on speed and the tactical advantage chariots provided on an open battlefield. The biblical writer may mention this here since the battle against Deborah and the Israelites would be fought in a riverbed. There the tactical advantage was taken away, and the weight of the iron chariots would cause them to be stuck in the mud, taking away their speed. The biblical writer may also refer to the size of Jabin's army in order to highlight the miraculous nature of God's defeat of such an impressive foe. Sisera and Jabin ruled and oppressed Israel for twenty years, and the people called for God to help them.

Deborah Speaks for God (4:4–7)

Deborah was an important leader as both a prophetess and judge in Israel. It is important to note that Deborah held this leadership role in the community prior to the events in the Book of Judges. It seems clear from the story that she had built a reputation as a wise leader and served in that role for years. Everybody knew that she was a prophet of God, and they came to her for answers to their questions and to resolve their disputes.

Many are surprised by the position held by Deborah because it is often assumed women in ancient Israel were not able to hold such positions and were fully dependent on and subject to the leadership of their husbands. Yet notice the way verse 4 describes Deborah as "a prophetess, the wife of Lappidoth." The order is significant. Before her husband is mentioned, we learn about her role as a spokesperson for God. That role is then further emphasized by the note that she was judging Israel at the time Jabin was ruling Israel. It should also be noted that no one in the story seems to have had an issue with her gender.

Deborah Leads the People (4:8–16)

Barak was the recognized leader of Israel's army. He had likely led his soldiers into many battles before. Deborah went to meet Barak and told him to take 10,000 soldiers to fight Sisera. She told him this was what God wanted him to do, and God would go with him and help him defeat Israel's enemy.

God essentially told Barak all he had to do was lead the army to the battlefield and watch how God would secure the victory. Barak, however, was hesitant. Even after hearing God's plan for the battle and assurance of victory, Barak appeared to have more faith in Deborah than in God. His thinking was apparently limited by what he thought was possible, and he did not see how 10,000 Israelites could possibly defeat an army that included 900 chariots. He seemed to have a great deal of confidence in Deborah as he made her accompanying him a condition of his leading the army. Perhaps he wanted her to lead so she could take the blame when they were defeated. Yet his trust should have been placed in the words Deborah spoke rather than in her presence.

Because of this lack of faith on the part of Barak, he would be denied any acclaim for the coming victory. Instead the credit would go to a woman whom the reader naturally assumes will be Deborah. Barak needed to understand that strong leadership does not question or place conditions on the call of God, but is simply ready to step forward and move ahead when the call comes.

Once they arrived on the battlefield, it was Deborah who gave the call to action by simply reminding Barak and all the army that God had already gone ahead of them and secured the victory. They simply needed to proceed and overtake Sisera's soldiers. The writer described the entire battle in very few words in verses 15–16. The brevity of the description adds to the sense of the brevity of the fighting. In fact, there appeared to have been very little fighting as Sisera's army seemed surprised by the attack and was easily routed. There is a fuller description of what happened in Judges 5:19–23. As Sisera's army was crossing the Kishon River, a flash flood rushed upon them, embedding chariot wheels in the mud and sweeping away many of Sisera's men, leaving the remainder in confusion and panic. At the sight of this chaotic scene, Sisera fled.

As Sisera ran, he came to the tent of a man named Heber the Kenite and his wife Jael (Judges 4:17–22). Seeing Sisera, Jael invited him inside to rest. She offered him food and drink and a place to lie down. Once Sisera was asleep, Jael killed him by driving a tent stake through his temple and into the ground. She then informed Barak that his enemy was dead and showed him where the body was. Thus Jael fulfilled the words Deborah had spoken concerning the credit for the defeat of the Canaanites going to a woman.

Deborah's Leadership Is Remembered (5:1–7)

Chapter 5 is a poetic account of the battle between Deborah and Barak on one side and Jabin and Sisera on the other.

While it appears this poem was written by Deborah, it is possible that it was remembered and recited by later generations as a reminder of how God had used Deborah to bring victory over Israel's enemy. While the poem is a reminder that even great leaders need God's help, God is able to work only as individuals step forward and allow God to work through them to lead his people. In this case, although God had initially called Barak to lead, it was Deborah who is remembered because of her willingness to exercise the leadership that the people needed to accomplish God's plans.

Deborah is referred to as a "mother in Israel" in verse 7. This is not only a reminder of her leadership, but it also says much about the type of leadership Deborah exercised. She did not rule over them or make demands. She simply stated God's desire and plan and called them to follow. Deborah shows us that exercising strong godly leadership does not mean ruling over people. It simply means listening to God, trusting his guidance, and helping others to see and follow God as well.

Implications for Today

God has specifically and uniquely gifted all believers with particular spiritual gifts. Those gifts are given to be used in strengthening the church for ministry. Because of this, each believer is called to actively use whatever her or his gifts may be in service. God gives these gifts without regard to social or economic status, race, or gender. Believers should never place limits or restrictions on how or by whom certain gifts may be used, but should encourage and assist everyone in finding opportunities to honor God by using their gifts wherever God may lead them to do so.

BAPTIST WOMEN

In recent years, Baptist attitudes toward church leadership roles for women often have unfortunately been seen as suppressive and limiting. Yet it was not always this way. Early Baptist churches in the 1600s in England routinely had women as deacons and elders.[1] Too, women such as Martha Stearns Marshall, an eighteenth-century Baptist leader, were highly sought after to preach in Baptist churches in the United States, especially in the South.

Baptist women have especially been influential in establishing and leading missions' organizations, and missions' offerings are named for women. Moves to limit roles for women seem to have been connected to, among other things, an adverse reaction to the women's suffrage movement and a change in church structure to provide what was considered to be more *acceptable roles* for women. Many Baptist churches today are more open to leadership roles for women.

Helps for Leaders

While not everyone is called to be a pastor, all believers are called to actively participate in the life and mission of the church. Here are some helps for you to take a leadership role within the church.

- Identify your particular spiritual gift
- Pray for God's wisdom and guidance
- Look for a specific ministry through which you could use your gift (This may involve starting a new ministry in your area.)
- Seek others with similar gifts and encourage them to join you

QUESTIONS

1. Can you think of a time when you trusted a person more than you trusted God? What happened?

LESSON 6: *Deborah*

2. Who are some great women leaders you know? What makes them great leaders?

3. Should women be allowed to be leaders in the church? Why or why not?

4. Are there areas of ministry you could lead? What are they?

5. What would it take for you to exercise leadership in your local church?

NOTES

1. See www.baptisthistory.org/contissues/deweese3.htm, www.baptisthistory.org/bhhs/21stcentury/womendeacons.html, http://baptisthistory.org/contissues/huffman.htm. All accessed 1/6/2011. See also Leon McBeth, *Women in Baptist Life* (Nashville, Tennessee: Broadman Press, 1979).

FOCAL TEXT
1 Samuel 12:1–5, 13–25

BACKGROUND
1 Samuel 8; 11—12

LESSON SEVEN

Samuel:
Being Faithful to the Highest Allegiance

MAIN IDEA

Samuel asserted that he had been fully faithful to the Lord and warned the people that they too must serve the Lord faithfully with all their heart.

QUESTION TO EXPLORE

In practice, where do you place the highest allegiance of your life?

STUDY AIM

To identify key elements in how Samuel gave his highest allegiance to God and encouraged the people to do the same, and to decide on ways I will express my highest allegiance to God

QUICK READ

After years of being their leader, Samuel had anointed a king to rule over Israel. Having done so, he stood before the people and reminded them that the highest allegiance of the people and the king was to God.

One of my favorite memories of childhood is going to Vacation Bible School each year. Those who went as children or who helped lead as adults will remember that during the opening assembly each day, the children recited the Pledge of Allegiance to the American flag, to the Christian flag, and to the Bible.

We either explicitly or implicitly pledge allegiance to many things in our lives. In addition to the three already mentioned, we also pledge allegiance to our spouse and perhaps to our school and our employer. Such pledges are important. They are an expression of who we are and what we value. They help provide direction by placing boundaries on our words and actions and helping us set our priorities. Yet with so many things to which we pledge allegiance, one must ask, *Which one is the most important?* In the direst of circumstances, which would we cling to the tightest? Which person or thing should get our highest allegiance?

The time of the judges had been disastrous for the people of Israel. The cycle of sin-judgment-repentance-deliverance that had characterized the early chapters of the Book of Judges had gradually collapsed until the Israelites found themselves killing one another at the end of the book, at which point Samuel entered the story.

Samuel served an important and unique role as a bridge between the period of the judges and the monarchy. He was effectively the last judge and the one whom God called to anoint Israel's first two kings. In this role he sought to lead the people from the rampant sin and idolatry we find at the end of the Book of Judges and back to full allegiance to God. When the people demanded an earthly king, Samuel opposed the idea and warned them of what a king would do and encouraged them to follow God as their king. When the people insisted, God led Samuel to anoint Saul as Israel's first king. Following Saul's first military victory as king, Samuel again called the people together to encourage them to place their allegiance in God instead of earthly leaders.

1 Samuel 12:1–5, 13–25

1 Then Samuel said to all Israel, "Behold, I have listened to your voice in all that you said to me and I have appointed a king over you. **2** "Now, here is the king walking before you, but I am old and gray, and behold my sons are with you. And I have walked before you from my youth even to this day. **3** "Here I am; bear witness against me before the Lord and His anointed. Whose ox have I taken, or whose donkey have I taken, or whom have I defrauded? Whom have I oppressed, or from whose hand have I taken a bribe to blind my eyes with it? I will restore it to you." **4** They said, "You have not defrauded us or oppressed us or taken anything from any man's hand." **5** He said to them, "The Lord is witness against you, and His anointed is witness this day that you have found nothing in my hand." And they said, "He is witness."

• •

13 "Now therefore, here is the king whom you have chosen, whom you have asked for, and behold, the Lord has set a king over you. **14** "If you will fear the Lord and serve Him, and listen to His voice and not rebel against the command of the Lord, then both you and also the king who reigns over you will follow the Lord your God. **15** "If you will not listen to the voice of the Lord, but rebel against the command of the Lord, then the hand of the Lord will be against you, as it was against your fathers. **16** "Even now, take your stand and see this great thing which the Lord will do before your eyes. **17** "Is it not the wheat harvest today? I will call to the Lord, that He may send thunder and rain. Then you will know and see that your wickedness is great which you have done in the sight of the Lord by asking for yourselves a king." **18** So Samuel called to the Lord, and the Lord sent thunder and rain that day; and all the people greatly feared the Lord and Samuel. **19** Then all the people said to Samuel, "Pray for your servants to the Lord your God, so that we may not die, for we have added to all our sins this evil by asking for ourselves a king." **20** Samuel said to the people, "Do not fear. You have committed all this evil, yet do not turn aside from following the Lord, but serve the Lord with all your heart. **21** "You must not turn aside, for then you would go after futile things which can not profit or deliver, because they are futile. **22** "For the Lord will not abandon His people on account of His great name, because the Lord has been pleased to make you a people for Himself. **23** "Moreover, as for me, far be it from me that I should sin against the LORD by ceasing to pray for you; but I will instruct you in the good and right way. **24** "Only fear the LORD and serve Him in truth with all your heart; for consider what great things He has done for you. **25** "But if you still do wickedly, both you and your king will be swept away."

Demonstrating Allegiance to the Lord (12:1–5)

After Samuel had anointed Saul king, the Ammonites attacked Jabesh-Gilead (1 Samuel 11). The leaders of the city called for the rest of the Israelites to help them. Saul gathered a large army and defeated the Ammonites. The people then gathered at Gilgal to affirm Saul as their king. In 1 Samuel 11:12–15 we learn that apparently some had questioned whether Saul should be their king. When the crowd called for the death of those doubters, Saul quickly intervened and focused their attention on the victory God had won for them. Samuel then stood before the people to turn the leadership of the people over to Saul and to warn the people again that their highest allegiance was still to God.

Samuel began by pointing out he was now an old man, and both Saul and Samuel's sons were now in positions to lead the people. Samuel had completed all the work the people had asked him to do, and it was time for him to step aside. Samuel reminded the people of the kind of leader he had been. He stated he had never cheated or taken anything from anyone. He had never accepted a bribe or used his position of authority to oppress anyone. Samuel had always tried to lead the way God wanted him to lead. He had modeled for the people what it meant to follow God above all else. He challenged anyone to show when or how he had been dishonest or a poor leader. There may be a subtle reminder in these words of his earlier warning in chapter 8 concerning what a king would do. There he had warned that a king would take their land and children as well as impose taxes on them. He may have been drawing a contrast between what they were giving up and what they were getting as a challenge to make sure any future king did what was right before God and help the people to follow God. God was still their true king and they needed to put their trust in God above any earthly king.

To emphasize this even further, in verses 6–12 Samuel reminded the people of their own history and the many ways God had led them and provided for them. He told them that, even though Moses and Aaron had led them out of Egypt and through the desert, it was God who had delivered them and given them the land they were now living in. It was God who, through his grace, had heard the cries of the people in Egypt and had raised up Moses and Aaron to be his leaders. He reminded them how God had continually delivered them from their enemies during the time of the judges. It was the people who had then demanded a king even though God had been their king.

Despite all God had done for them, the people had finally rejected God's leadership in exchange for a king in order to be like everyone else.

Calling for Allegiance to the Lord (12:13–18)

Having stated his case, Samuel called on the people to maintain their allegiance to God. Even though they would have an earthly king, their highest devotion was to God. They must live according to their covenant with God above obedience to any king. In verse 14, Samuel pointed out that allegiance to God was not only expected of the people, but also of the king as well. As long as the king and the people maintained their commitment to God above all else, life would go well for them, and God would continue to bless them. If the people or the king should turn away from following God, God would turn his hand against them and punish their disobedience.

As punishment on the people for rejecting God and asking for a king, God sent a powerful thunderstorm. With the heavy rains, the storm would likely have done damage to the crops that were ready for harvest and thus would have been seen as a punishment. This storm would have also been a demonstration of the punishment God would send as judgment for future sin. Such a storm would have been unusual for that time of year and would thus clearly display God's power by demonstrating his authority over nature. The people should thus understand that God's words were not to be taken lightly as an empty threat. In addition, such a powerful God would certainly be worthy of the people's allegiance and obedience and would certainly be more than able to fulfill his words of both blessing and punishment. When the people saw the rain and heard the thunder, they were afraid.

Encouraging Allegiance to the Lord (12:19–25)

In their fear, the people asked Samuel to pray to God to stop the rain before they perished. Notice in verse 19, however, that the people told Samuel to pray to "your" God. The people still did not seem to understand that God was their God. God wanted each person to know him individually. Yet the people acknowledged their sin. They not only saw the sin in asking for a king, but they also admitted that they were guilty of past sins as well. Samuel could easily see and understand their fear. He likely knew that if the people became focused on their fear, they would miss the point. In verse 20, Samuel sought to calm their fears. God did not want the people to live in fear but in personal relationship with him. Samuel told them that even though they had sinned, God would not destroy them as long as they would not turn away from God. He assured them that since God had made a covenant with them and established them as a people, he would never forsake them. The Israelites bore God's name, and God would never allow dishonor to come to that name by violating his promises.

Samuel then assured the people that, even though he would no longer be their leader, they could know that he would continue to pray for them. He stated it would in fact be sin on his part if he should stop praying for their spiritual commitment to God. How would it affect our personal prayers if we were to have this same perspective?

Samuel also promised he would still be active among them, seeking to instruct them in how to fulfill their allegiance to God. Although it is not stated explicitly, the implication is that this instruction would be directed to both the people and the king. Verses 24–25 conclude Samuel's speech by once again reemphasizing his primary warning and encouragement. He reminded them again that their highest allegiance was to the God who had done great things on their behalf. Thinking about God's many actions should motivate them to always serve God with all their hearts. Failure to do so would lead God to send judgment on the people and their king.

Implications for Today

Each of us fills a number of roles in life, such as family, work, and citizenship. In each of those roles, a number of people and things can call for our attention and devotion.

Many voices in our daily lives promise to lead us to fulfillment and happiness if we will simply devote ourselves to following them. While granting a measure of allegiance to many of these is acceptable, healthy, and often necessary, our ultimate allegiance should always be to God. As believers we are also called to encourage and pray for one another that we may be able to maintain that allegiance. God has blessed each person in many ways, and as we pledge our highest allegiance to God, he brings true fulfillment to our life.

The Attraction of Idols

As we read the pages of the Old Testament, we may find ourselves wondering why the Israelites often seemed to return to worshiping idols even after God warned them and sent judgment on them. What was the attraction of worshiping these false gods? Several things may have played a part in this. First, idols gave people a sense of being in control. They could move the god wherever they wanted, and as long as they performed the right rituals, the god was obligated to bless them. Second, idols gave the people a physical object to focus on when worshiping. In the ancient world, it could be difficult to worship an invisible god. Finally, the false gods did not place moral requirements on the people. They simply demanded worship regardless of how a person lived or what other gods he or she might worship. Yet before we criticize them too harshly, we should realize that we too have things we worship for the same reasons even though they might not be in the form of idols made of wood.

CHARACTERISTICS OF ALLEGIANCE TO GOD

As we examine Samuel's speech to the people, we can identify characteristics of allegiance to God.

- While allegiance to God is a personal matter, it affects the ways we treat one another.
- Praying for and challenging others to maintain their allegiance to God helps us to strengthen our own allegiance.
- Recognizing and remembering God's leadership and provisions can motivate us to live out our commitment.
- We perhaps most clearly demonstrate our allegiance to God when we follow where God leads even when we do not understand or agree.

QUESTIONS

1. Samuel had to deal with a change in his role as leader. How can we deal with changes in leadership?

2. How can we always be sure to give God our highest allegiance?

LESSON 7: *Samuel*

3. What are some characteristics of good leaders?

4. Is there a time when you were hesitant to follow God's leading? What happened?

FOCAL TEXT
2 Samuel 11:2–15; 12:1–13a

BACKGROUND
2 Samuel 11—12

LESSON EIGHT

David and Nathan:
Accepting Personal Responsibility for Sin

MAIN IDEA

When challenged by Nathan, God's prophet, David the king accepted personal responsibility for his heinous sins, confessing he had sinned against God.

QUESTION TO EXPLORE

Why are people often reluctant to accept personal responsibility for their sin?

STUDY AIM

To state why every person must accept personal responsibility for his or her own sins and to decide how I need to respond to this truth

QUICK READ

King David committed adultery with Bathsheba. After learning Bathsheba had conceived, David had her husband killed in battle. God told the prophet Nathan to confront David about his sins.

According to an often-told story of how spider monkeys are captured, hunters place containers with narrow openings in areas populated by spider monkeys and fill the containers with nuts. The openings are large enough for the monkeys to reach into but too small for them to pull their hand out while holding a nut. According to the story, the monkeys come along, reach in to get a nut, and then are caught when they refuse to let go in order to get free. While this story may not be completely accurate, it illustrates well the danger of temptation.

We live in a world full of temptations. Some may seem rather harmless while others have clear and often devastating consequences. Some involve a one-time act while others can become lifetime habits. Some have no attraction for some people while others find those same things difficult to resist. Whatever the particular temptation, often it can be difficult to let go even when we see the results. Because of this and the associated guilt, we most often try to deny and hide our actions whenever we give in to the temptation. Yet God knows each and every word and deed and requires we accept personal responsibility for our sins so we can confess them and experience forgiveness. The story of David's affair with Bathsheba shows us how easy it can be to give in to temptation and the consequences we face when we fail to take responsibility.

LESSON 8: *David and Nathan*

2 SAMUEL 11:2–15

2 Now when evening came David arose from his bed and walked around on the roof of the king's house, and from the roof he saw a woman bathing; and the woman was very beautiful in appearance. **3** So David sent and inquired about the woman. And one said, "Is this not Bathsheba, the daughter of Eliam, the wife of Uriah the Hittite?" **4** David sent messengers and took her, and when she came to him, he lay with her; and when she had purified herself from her uncleanness, she returned to her house. **5** The woman conceived; and she sent and told David, and said, "I am pregnant." **6** Then David sent to Joab, saying, "Send me Uriah the Hittite." So Joab sent Uriah to David. **7** When Uriah came to him, David asked concerning the welfare of Joab and the people and the state of the war. **8** Then David said to Uriah, "Go down to your house, and wash your feet." And Uriah went out of the king's house, and a present from the king was sent out after him. **9** But Uriah slept at the door of the king's house with all the servants of his lord, and did not go down to his house. **10** Now when they told David, saying, "Uriah did not go down to his house," David said to Uriah, "Have you not come from a journey? Why did you not go down to your house?" **11** Uriah said to David, "The ark and Israel and Judah are staying in temporary shelters, and my lord Joab and the servants of my lord are camping in the open field. Shall I then go to my house to eat and to drink and to lie with my wife? By your life and the life of your soul, I will not do this thing." **12** Then David said to Uriah, "Stay here today also, and tomorrow I will let you go." So Uriah remained in Jerusalem that day and the next. **13** Now David called him, and he ate and drank before him, and he made him drunk; and in the evening he went out to lie on his bed with his lord's servants, but he did not go down to his house. **14** Now in the morning David wrote a letter to Joab and sent it by the hand of Uriah. **15** He had written in the letter, saying, "Place Uriah in the front line of the fiercest battle and withdraw from him, so that he may be struck down and die."

2 Samuel 12:1–13a

1 Then the Lord sent Nathan to David. And he came to him and said, "There were two men in one city, the one rich and the other poor. **2** "The rich man had a great many flocks and herds. **3** "But the poor man had nothing except one little ewe lamb Which he bought and nourished; And it grew up together with him and his children. It would eat of his bread and drink of his cup and lie in his bosom, And was like a daughter to him. **4** "Now a traveler came to the rich man, And he was unwilling to take from his own flock or his own herd, To prepare for the wayfarer who had come to him; Rather he took the poor man's ewe lamb and prepared it for the man who had come to him." **5** Then David's anger burned greatly against the man, and he said to Nathan, "As

LESSON 8: *David and Nathan*

the LORD lives, surely the man who has done this deserves to die. **6** "He must make restitution for the lamb fourfold, because he did this thing and had no compassion." **7** Nathan then said to David, "You are the man! Thus says the LORD God of Israel, 'It is I who anointed you king over Israel and it is I who delivered you from the hand of Saul. **8** 'I also gave you your master's house and your master's wives into your care, and I gave you the house of Israel and Judah; and if that had been too little, I would have added to you many more things like these! **9** 'Why have you despised the word of the LORD by doing evil in His sight? You have struck down Uriah the Hittite with the sword, have taken his wife to be your wife, and have killed him with the sword of the sons of Ammon. **10** 'Now therefore, the sword shall never depart from your house, because you have despised Me and have taken the wife of Uriah the Hittite to be your wife.' **11** "Thus says the LORD, 'Behold, I will raise up evil against you from your own household; I will even take your wives before your eyes and give them to your companion, and he will lie with your wives in broad daylight. **12** 'Indeed you did it secretly, but I will do this thing before all Israel, and under the sun.'" **13** Then David said to Nathan, "I have sinned against the LORD."

David's Initial Sin (11:2–5)

Following Saul's failure as king, God called Samuel to anoint David as the next king of Israel. The early years of David's reign had been marked by great success. He had led the people to numerous victories over their enemies and always remembered to give the glory to God. Although David was prohibited from building God's temple, God had made a covenant with David stating his descendants would always reign on the throne in Jerusalem.

Then at the beginning of 2 Samuel 11, David sent his army to fight while he stayed in Jerusalem. Many have suggested David should have been on the battlefield with the army. Yet this was not the first time David had stayed behind (2 Samuel 10:7), and it was certainly not unusual for a king not to accompany his troops into battle in order to attend to other duties of a king. The problem was not where David was, but what David was doing. Verse 2 indicates David had been lying on his bed into the late afternoon. While there is nothing wrong with regular rest, it is often in times of leisure that temptations can more easily come upon us.

Notice the numerous active verbs about David's actions in verses 2–5: David "arose," "walked," "saw," "sent," "inquired," "sent," "took," "lay." Such an accumulation of verbs indicates David was an active participant in this sin. He could not claim to have been a passive and innocent victim. How often do we try to excuse or pass the blame for our sin? The rapid succession of these verbs also demonstrates how quickly temptation leads to sin and its consequences when we fail to take a stand against it. David clearly could have stopped the progression at any point simply by refusing to take the next step.

After inquiring about the identity of the woman, David learned she was the daughter of Eliam and the wife of Uriah. According to 2 Samuel 23:34, Eliam was one of David's close friends who had helped him during the years he was running from Saul. The fact that Uriah's house was close enough to the palace that David was able to see Bathsheba on her roof indicates Uriah was a trusted military leader. Only such trusted advisors or leaders would own houses close to the palace. Yet even after learning Bathsheba was the daughter of a close friend and the wife of a trusted military leader, David continued to pursue her. Each step took David further away from God's plan and closer to more serious consequences and punishment. Verse 5 reports Bathsheba conceived a child. The fact that she "purified herself from her uncleanness" left no doubt David was indeed the father.

David's Attempted Cover-up (11:6–15)

After this first sin, David had two choices. He could confess his sin and ask God for forgiveness or he could try to hide his sin. David decided to hide his affair by calling Uriah back from the battlefield.

Uriah was a Hittite. In the Old Testament, this term seems to refer to one of two different groups. The Hittite

Empire had existed in what is now Syria during the time of Moses, Joshua, and the judges. Another group of Hittites had settled in the area of Hebron prior to Israel's entry into Canaan and were not removed from the land by Joshua. Uriah seems to have been from this latter group.

David wanted Uriah to give a report of the battle and then go home and sleep with his wife. The phrase "wash your feet" in verse 8 was a Hebrew euphemism for sexual intercourse. Thus everyone would assume Uriah was the father of the child. Uriah however, refused to enjoy the comforts of his home as long as his fellow soldiers were on the battlefield. Even after David got Uriah drunk, he refused to go into his house but "slept at the door of the king's house." Thus this non-Israelite acted far more nobly than did David, a man described as one after God's own heart. David here had another opportunity to confess and seek to resolve the situation appropriately. David, however, did not seek God's forgiveness or help. His desires led him further into sin as he schemed to have Uriah killed.

David gave Uriah a note to take to Joab on the frontline of the battle. Joab was David's most trusted and loyal friend and general. Joab had been with David for many years and had assisted him in his fight with Saul. David knew Joab would do whatever David asked. The note instructed Joab to place Uriah at the front of the battle. When the fighting got intense, Joab and the army should withdraw and allow Uriah to be killed.

According to verses 16–17, Joab carried out David's instructions, and Uriah was killed. Joab then sent a messenger to report all had happened to David. David sent a message back to Joab telling him not to be upset. Both sides of a battle lose soldiers. Joab should strengthen the army and press the attack on the city until they conquered it. David almost certainly must have thought his secret was safe and no one would ever know about his sin.

God's Judgment (12:1–13)

Nathan was a prophet of God and a trusted advisor to David. It was Nathan who had told David about God's covenant with David and his descendants in 2 Samuel 7. God told Nathan about David's sins and instructed him to confront David. Nathan began by telling David a story of two men. One was a rich man who owned many sheep, and yet he had stolen the only lamb of a poor neighbor to feed his guests. The story was intended as a parable concerning David's sin. Had he been listening closely, David might have picked up on the meaning behind the story. In verse 3, Nathan says the lamb was "like a daughter" to the poor man. The Hebrew word for "daughter" is *bath*, which forms the first part of Bathsheba's name. David had many wives, but he had taken the wife of someone else. David thus did what Samuel warned the people a king would do in taking their daughters into the palace (1 Samuel 8:13).

After telling his story, Nathan asked David what should be done to the rich man. David apparently did not understand the true meaning of the story, for he stated that the rich man must give the poor man four sheep to replace the one stolen. David here was imposing the exact punishment dictated by the law in Exodus 22:1.

Having heard David pronounce the punishment, Nathan told David that David himself was the rich man and God was going to punish him for his sins. It seems part of David's problem was he had forgotten it was God who had raised him to his position as king. Notice in verses 7–8 God used "I" four times to remind David God had greatly blessed him. God knew about all David's sins and would punish him. Since David had put Uriah to the sword, a sword would never depart from David's house. David would face turmoil within his own family for the rest of his life, and his wives would be taken from him. Although David had tried to commit his sins in secret, everyone would see God's punishment on him. David had thought he could do whatever he wanted without anyone knowing. Yet God had seen everything David did.

Verse 13 reports that David was truly sorry for his sins and confessed his guilt. God heard David's confession and forgave him. Because David had confessed, God allowed him to live and remain king. The son conceived by Bathsheba, however, would die. David accepted personal responsibility for his sin and God forgave him. Psalm 51 provides us with deeper insight into David's acknowledgment of his sin and helps us to learn more about what it means to take personal responsibility for our sins.

Implications for Today

Each of us faces a multitude of temptations every day. Many are easy to recognize while others are much more subtle. Regardless of the size or strength of the temptation, they all are designed to distract us from following God's path and weakening our witness. Today the internet and other technological advances have greatly multiplied the temptations and made many things much more accessible than before. Because of this, it can often seem easy to hide or even excuse giving in to temptation when it happens in the privacy of our homes and when it appears that no one gets hurt. Yet the Bible is clear that whenever and wherever we yield to temptation, we sin. We must recognize yielding to temptation for what it is and take responsibility before God for our action. Only then can God forgive us and restore us to fellowship.

FROM TEMPTATION TO SIN

How often have you heard or said, *The devil made me do it*? The statement is simply not true. The devil does not have the power to force anyone to do anything. Yet sometimes a particular temptation can seem so strong we feel powerless against it. Regardless of the strength or specific object of the temptation, each person has a choice of whether or not to give in, however.

Temptation is not sin but merely the opportunity for sin. Temptation only becomes sin as we choose to participate in the object of the temptation. Sometimes when a particular sin has become a habit, we may not be aware we have made a choice, but whenever Satan presents us with some temptation, we have the power to choose. And each person is held responsible for his or her choice in the face of whatever temptation comes (1 Corinthians 10:13; James 1:13–15).

Dealing with Temptation

With so many temptations around us, how can we deal with temptations and avoid sin? Consider these ways:

- Understand that temptation is not sin and refuse to feel guilty about being tempted.
- Recognize that most temptations will be subtle and will seek to entice you to make small compromises.
- Remember that God did not send the temptation and has already provided a way to overcome it.
- Maintain a daily time of Bible study and prayer so you will be equipped to recognize and withstand

LESSON 8: *David and Nathan*

temptation. The time to deal with temptation is long before the moment of temptation.

- When you sin, refuse to make excuses. Confess the sin and ask God to forgive.

QUESTIONS

1. In addition to reading the Bible and prayer, what can we do to avoid or resist temptations?

2. What part of this lesson has been the most challenging for you? Why?

3. Why is it important to take personal responsibility for our sin?

FOCAL TEXT
Amos 1:1–2; 2:6–16; 7:10–17

BACKGROUND
Amos 1—2; 7

LESSON NINE

Amos:
Facing Opposition Courageously

MAIN IDEA

Although Amos had no professional religious authority, he spoke God's message of judgment courageously in spite of opposition.

QUESTION TO EXPLORE

Whose voice gets most of your attention?

STUDY AIM

To analyze how Amos courageously served God and to identify ways in which I need to respond to God's call

QUICK READ

Despite intense opposition and lack of professional credentials, the prophet Amos courageously delivered God's message of judgment to Israel.

T. B. Maston was a unique Baptist prophet. He was neither a preacher nor a pastor. He was a seminary professor who did his prophetic work through teaching and writing. When I began my studies at Southwestern Baptist Theological Seminary in the late 1970s, Maston was still writing but had retired from teaching. In my second year at Southwestern, the library put up a display that commemorated his work on racial desegregation in the 1950s and 60s. Maston was an early proponent of racial equality and desegregation, advocating positions contrary to his culture, its laws, and his denomination. The display included letters he received from fellow Baptists, attacking him for his stands. They accused him of being unbiblical, un-Christian, and un-American for saying that blacks and whites had equal rights. Some of them even commended prominent Southern Baptist pastors who advocated segregation. Like most prophets, Maston suffered severe criticism and ridicule for bringing God's message.

Today's lesson is about another unique prophet: Amos. Amos was unique in that he was neither a professional prophet nor a student in a prophetic school. He was a shepherd and a dresser of sycamore-fig trees. Despite his lack of professional prophetic credentials, he brought God's message to his people and experienced fierce opposition for doing so.

Amos 1:1–2

1 The words of Amos, one of the shepherds of Tekoa—what he saw concerning Israel two years before the earthquake, when Uzziah was king of Judah and Jeroboam son of Jehoash was king of Israel. **2** He said:
"The Lord roars from Zion
   and thunders from Jerusalem;
   the pastures of the shepherds dry up,
   and the top of Carmel withers."

Amos 2:6–16

6 This is what the Lord says:
"For three sins of Israel,
   even for four, I will not turn back my wrath.
They sell the righteous for silver,
   and the needy for a pair of sandals.
7 They trample on the heads of the poor
   as upon the dust of the ground
   and deny justice to the oppressed.
Father and son use the same girl
   and so profane my holy name.
8 They lie down beside every altar
   on garments taken in pledge.
In the house of their god
   they drink wine taken as fines.

⁹ "I destroyed the Amorite before them,
  though he was tall as the cedars
  and strong as the oaks.
I destroyed his fruit above
  and his roots below.
¹⁰ "I brought you up out of Egypt,
  and I led you forty years in the desert
  to give you the land of the Amorites.
¹¹ I also raised up prophets from among your sons
  and Nazirites from among your young men.
Is this not true, people of Israel?"
        declares the LORD.
¹² "But you made the Nazirites drink wine
  and commanded the prophets not to prophesy.
¹³ "Now then, I will crush you
  as a cart crushes when loaded with grain.
¹⁴ The swift will not escape,
  the strong will not muster their strength,
  and the warrior will not save his life.
¹⁵ The archer will not stand his ground,
  the fleet-footed soldier will not get away,
  and the horseman will not save his life.
¹⁶ Even the bravest warriors
  will flee naked on that day,"
        declares the LORD.

Amos 7:10–17

10 Then Amaziah the priest of Bethel sent a message to Jeroboam king of Israel: "Amos is raising a conspiracy against you in the very heart of Israel. The land cannot bear all his words. **11** For this is what Amos is saying:

> "'Jeroboam will die by the sword,
> and Israel will surely go into exile,
> away from their native land.'"

12 Then Amaziah said to Amos, "Get out, you seer! Go back to the land of Judah. Earn your bread there and do your prophesying there. **13** Don't prophesy anymore at Bethel, because this is the king's sanctuary and the temple of the kingdom."

14 Amos answered Amaziah, "I was neither a prophet nor a prophet's son, but I was a shepherd, and I also took care of sycamore-fig trees. **15** But the Lord took me from tending the flock and said to me, 'Go, prophesy to my people Israel.' **16** Now then, hear the word of the Lord. You say,

> "'Do not prophesy against Israel,
> and stop preaching against the house of Isaac.'

17 "Therefore this is what the Lord says:

> "'Your wife will become a prostitute in the city,
> and your sons and daughters will fall by the sword.
> Your land will be measured and divided up,
> and you yourself will die in a pagan country.
> And Israel will certainly go into exile,
> away from their native land.'"

The Lord Thunders Through the Prophet (1:1–2)

The first verse of the Book of Amos describes the prophet as "one of the shepherds of Tekoa."[1] Tekoa, a small village, was located about six miles south of Bethlehem. Since Amos prophesied at Bethel (see Amos 7:13), he, a resident of the kingdom of Judah, had traveled to the kingdom of Israel to prophesy against it.

The term "shepherd" is ambiguous. Amos could have been a poor shepherd or a wealthy person who owned sheep. Amos 7:14 adds that he was a dresser of sycamore-fig trees. Workers had to slit the fruit of these trees just before they ripened to make them edible. In this verse, Amos stated he was neither a prophet nor a prophet's son. He probably meant he was neither a professional prophet nor a member of a prophetic school. Many gained a living by prophesying, and some of them were members of prophetic schools called "sons of the prophets" (see 1 Kings 20:35). The members of these schools were disciples of prominent prophets.

Amos prophesied during the reigns of Uzziah, king of Judah, and Jeroboam (II), king of Israel (Amos 1:1). He ministered during the time of the divided kingdoms, around the middle of the eighth century B.C. One of the great arguments between these kingdoms concerned the proper place of worship. The temple of the Lord was on Mount Zion in Jerusalem, but the first king of Israel (Jeroboam I) had established a sanctuary at Bethel (see

1 Kings 12:32). Amos made it clear where the Lord was when he said that the Lord roared from Zion and thundered from Jerusalem (Amos 1:2). Imagine the reception Amos received when he uttered these words at Bethel. It was a direct repudiation of that sanctuary.

If you've ever heard the roar of a lion, you know it's impressive and intimidating. Thunder is even more impressive. Amos said the Lord was pronouncing his powerful word that would produce judgment on the world, including Israel. When God's powerful word went out, the rich pastures dried up and the top of Carmel withered. Carmel was a mountain in the Northern kingdom, but sometimes writers used the word to refer to the region of the mountain. Using few words, Amos described God's judgment going forth in great power.

Although Amos lacked prophetic credentials in terms of income and training, he brought the word of a great God who was about to act powerfully in the world. In the verses that follow (1:3—2:16), Amos used a remarkable rhetorical device to get his hearers' attention and dramatize his message. He delighted his Israelite hearers when he began by proclaiming his judgment on their neighbors. Each time, he used the expression, "for three sins . . . , even for four." The idea was that three sins would be more than sufficient cause for judgment, but four was completely over the top and made judgment sure. Amos told of judgment coming on the nations surrounding Israel, all the while working closer to Israel. It would be as if someone today stood in the United States and began pronouncing judgment on far-away nations like Russia and China, but worked closer to our country by speaking against Mexico and Canada. Even Amos's own country of Judah would face judgment (2:4–5). Finally, the prophet came to Israel (2:6) and essentially spent the rest of his prophecy pronouncing judgment against it.

Israel's Sins and God's Coming Judgment (2:6–16)

The primary reason for God's judgment against the Israelites was that they didn't fulfill the requirements of his covenant with them. He commanded them to worship him alone (Exodus 20:3–4), care for the poor (Exod. 22:26–27), and practice sexual morality (Leviticus 18:7–23). Yet they violated all these commands. They victimized the poor and the oppressed (Amos 2:6–7). They showed their attitudes toward the poor by taking garments they had taken from them in pledge and lying on them to worship idols and commit sexual immorality (2:8).

The Israelites turned away from God despite the fact he had loved and cared for them. When they settled in Canaan, he destroyed their fierce enemies (2:9). Prior to that, he delivered them from slavery in Egypt, and protected and guided them through the wilderness (2:10). He raised up prophets and Nazirites for the Israelites so they could receive his word (2:11).

The Israelites responded to God's goodness by making the Nazirites drink wine (2:12). Among the vows of the Nazirites was to refrain from drinking wine (see Numbers 6:1–4). The Israelites also commanded the prophets not to prophesy (Amos 2:12). In effect, they cut themselves off from God. For these reasons and more, they would face inescapable judgment for their sins (2:13–16). As a heavily-loaded cart crushes what it rolls over, God would crush his people. Even the swiftest and bravest warriors wouldn't escape.

These verses reveal God's revulsion at what was happening among his people. They violated his holy covenant with them. In doing so they grieved the God who had done so much for them. They also caused the poor and the oppressed to suffer. God had been patient, but he wasn't going to allow Israel's sin to continue.

As God's contemporary covenant people, these verses should remind us that we're accountable to him. He calls us to a distinctive lifestyle of love and righteousness, and holds us accountable to it. This text should also remind us that personal and social morality overlap. God was concerned about idolatry and sexual immorality, but he was also concerned about the oppression of the poor. These sins were equally important to him, and they should be the same to us.

Push-Back and Prophetic Courage (7:10–17)

Understandably, many Israelites took offense at Amos's words. This produced what we call today *push-back*. Amaziah, the high priest of Bethel, sent a message to King Jeroboam expressing his concern (7:10–11). In a wonderfully graphic expression, he said that "the land cannot bear all his words." Amos's unrelenting prophecies of judgment were demoralizing the people. Such words would be upsetting at any time, but ancient people believed that speaking words of judgment encouraged judgment to come. Words of blessing could bring blessing, and words of judgment could bring judgment. This cultural context made Amos's prophecies particularly distressing.

After sending his message to Jeroboam, Amaziah rebuked Amos. He derisively called Amos a "seer" and told him to go back to Judah and earn his living by prophesying there (Amos 7:12). He suggested Amos was a huckster. He commanded him not to prophesy anymore at Bethel because it was "the king's sanctuary and the temple of the kingdom." This rebuke shows that from Amaziah's perspective, Amos's prophesies were not only religiously offensive but also seditious. The Israelites blended religion and government, and so to attack the religious practices of the state was to attack the state itself.

The blending of religion and state was what led Jeroboam I to establish the sanctuary at Bethel. After he led a rebellion against King Solomon and established the

Northern kingdom, he knew that it would be bad for him politically if his people continued to go to Jerusalem to sacrifice at the temple. So he established a sanctuary at Bethel and put golden calves there. In the Old Testament's view, the establishment of this sanctuary accelerated Israel's lapse into idolatry (see 1 Kings 12:25–33).

Amos wasn't intimidated by Amaziah. He responded to his accusation of hucksterism by saying he wasn't a professional prophet or member of a prophetic school. Instead, he was a shepherd and a dresser of sycamore-fig trees whom God called to deliver his word to Israel (Amos 7:14–15). Instead of going away, Amos delivered a prophecy of judgment against Amaziah. He said that because Amaziah tried to silence him, his wife would become a prostitute and his children would be killed. He would lose his land and he would die in exile in a foreign land. These were the brutal realities of war in those days. Armies often divided families, carrying leaders off to exile as prizes, seizing their properties, killing their children, and selling their wives into prostitution. But Amaziah wouldn't be alone in his fate. All Israel would go into exile (7:16–17).

Despite the derision and strong opposition Amos received from a powerful figure like Amaziah, he stood his ground and delivered the message God gave him. In doing so, he challenged both the political and religious powers of Israel. In some ways, Amos's lack of professional prophetic credentials was a plus because Amaziah and others couldn't claim he was out for material gain.

Although he wasn't a religious professional, he traveled from his home and delivered a powerful prophecy because the Lord God called him to do it.

The word of the Lord often collides with political and religious powers. It requires tremendous faith and courage to bring that word when it does so. We see this collision in the story of Amos, but we can also see it in the stories of many other prophets of the Old Testament, and in those of Jesus and his followers in the New Testament.

For Life Today

God still calls us to bring his word to our world. Bringing a prophetic message is a joyous responsibility when it's good news. However, it's a fearsome task when it challenges political, religious, and cultural powers.

We need to remember a couple of important facts in relation to our prophetic responsibilities. First, our responsibility is to bring God's unadulterated, unvarnished word. When we know the word we're to bring will be unpopular or even offensive, we're tempted to water it down or *spin* it in a different direction. But our responsibility is to faithfully deliver God's message. Second, we find the strength to deliver that word through a strong relationship with God. The more rooted we are in the Father, the better able we are to weather criticism when it comes. Ultimately, we say with Peter and John that it is right in God's sight to obey him rather than human beings (Acts 4:19–20).

Prophets and Nazirites

The office of *prophet* is important in the Scriptures. Some prophets, like Elijah, lived on the frontiers of society, while others, like Nathan (lesson eight), were court prophets who received support from the king. The Scriptures also suggest that prophetic schools functioned in Israel. These prophetic schools were called "sons of the prophets" (see 1 Samuel 10:11; 1 Kings 20:35). Many prophets received material compensation for discerning God's will (see Numbers 22:7). When Amos said he was neither a prophet nor a son of a prophet (Amos 7:14), he probably meant he was neither a professional prophet nor a member of a prophetic school.

Nazirites were individuals who set themselves apart for special dedication to God. The word "Nazirite" comes from a Hebrew word meaning *separated* or *consecrated*. Numbers 6:1–21 describes the special discipline of Nazirites. This passage implies that most were Nazirites for a limed time, while some, like Samson (see Judges 13:5), took on this discipline for life. To make these individuals "drink wine" (Amos 2:12) was to corrupt them and turn them away from their consecration.

CASE STUDY

In a small Southern mill town in the 1930s, the workers of the mill were trying to form a union in order to get better wages and working conditions. The mill demanded all preachers in town preach against the union. The pastor of a small church who lived in a mill-owned home wasn't involved with the union, but he felt that it was wrong to preach against it. He had a wife and three children, and he knew that other preachers who hadn't followed the mill's orders had been evicted from their mill-owned homes. How should this pastor have responded?

QUESTIONS

1. How is God involved on the world stage today?

2. In what ways does God's great blessings on our country make us especially accountable to God for our actions and attitudes?

LESSON 9: *Amos*

3. What feelings do we have when we're in a situation in which we need to bring an unpopular prophetic word? Where do we find the strength and courage to bring that word?

4. What keeps us from speaking the prophetic message we know we need to speak?

5. Is there a prophetic word that your church needs to hear? Ask God for the power to deliver that word as he calls you.

NOTES

1. Unless otherwise indicated, all Scripture quotations in lessons 9–15 are from the New International Version.

FOCAL TEXT
1 Kings 22:6–28

BACKGROUND
1 Kings 22:1–40

LESSON TEN

Micaiah:
Telling the Hard Truth

MAIN IDEA

Micaiah courageously and faithfully spoke God's truth, even though it was unpopular and dangerous to do so.

QUESTION TO EXPLORE

What barriers must you overcome to speak the truth even when it is unpopular and even dangerous to do so?

STUDY AIM

To describe how Micaiah spoke truth to power even when doing so was unpopular and dangerous and to identify how to overcome barriers to speaking truth today when to do so is unpopular and even dangerous

QUICK READ

The prophet Micaiah spoke the truth about God's word to his king when all his fellow prophets did not. He suffered for telling the truth but was vindicated as a true prophet.

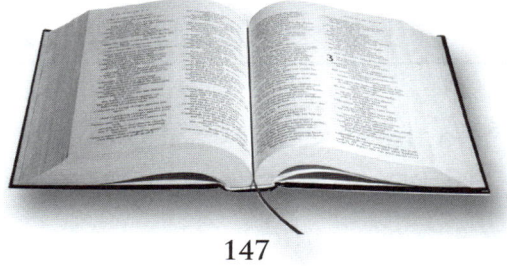

As Adolf Hitler rose in power in Germany in the early 1930s, many German Protestant Christians supported him. Calling themselves *German Christians*, they embraced anti-Semitism and a close relationship between church and state. Their efforts resulted in an unholy combination of nationalism, Aryanism, and Christianity. Yet not all Christians in Germany joined the movement. Pastors and Christian leaders like Martin Niemoller, Karl Barth, Dietrich Bonhoeffer, and others resisted it. They called themselves *confessing Christians* and stood against Hitler's control of the church. *Confessing Christians* were far less popular than *German Christians*.

Many German believers paid a high price for being *confessing Christians*. Some of them, like Niemoller, were sentenced to concentration camps. Others, like Barth, had to leave the country. Still others, like Bonhoeffer, were put to death.

This is just one historical example of people who spoke God's truth and experienced persecution for it. In this lesson, we consider the story of Micaiah, a true prophet of the Lord who suffered for bringing God's word but was vindicated as a true prophet.

1 Kings 22:6–28

6 So the king of Israel brought together the prophets—about four hundred men—and asked them, "Shall I go to war against Ramoth Gilead, or shall I refrain?"

LESSON 10: *Micaiah*

"Go," they answered, "for the Lord will give it into the king's hand."

⁷ But Jehoshaphat asked, "Is there not a prophet of the Lord here whom we can inquire of?"

⁸ The king of Israel answered Jehoshaphat, "There is still one man through whom we can inquire of the Lord, but I hate him because he never prophesies anything good about me, but always bad. He is Micaiah son of Imlah."

"The king should not say that," Jehoshaphat replied.

⁹ So the king of Israel called one of his officials and said, "Bring Micaiah son of Imlah at once."

¹⁰ Dressed in their royal robes, the king of Israel and Jehoshaphat king of Judah were sitting on their thrones at the threshing floor by the entrance of the gate of Samaria, with all the prophets prophesying before them. ¹¹ Now Zedekiah son of Kenaanah had made iron horns and he declared, "This is what the Lord says: 'With these you will gore the Arameans until they are destroyed.'"

¹² All the other prophets were prophesying the same thing. "Attack Ramoth Gilead and be victorious," they said, "for the Lord will give it into the king's hand."

¹³ The messenger who had gone to summon Micaiah said to him, "Look, as one man the other prophets are predicting success for the king. Let your word agree with theirs, and speak favorably."

¹⁴ But Micaiah said, "As surely as the Lord lives, I can tell him only what the Lord tells me."

¹⁵ When he arrived, the king asked him, "Micaiah, shall we go to war against Ramoth Gilead, or shall I refrain?"

"Attack and be victorious," he answered, "for the LORD will give it into the king's hand."

¹⁶ The king said to him, "How many times must I make you swear to tell me nothing but the truth in the name of the LORD?"

¹⁷ Then Micaiah answered, "I saw all Israel scattered on the hills like sheep without a shepherd, and the LORD said, 'These people have no master. Let each one go home in peace.'"

¹⁸ The king of Israel said to Jehoshaphat, "Didn't I tell you that he never prophesies anything good about me, but only bad?"

¹⁹ Micaiah continued, "Therefore hear the word of the LORD: I saw the LORD sitting on his throne with all the host of heaven standing around him on his right and on his left. ²⁰ And the LORD said, 'Who will entice Ahab into attacking Ramoth Gilead and going to his death there?'

"One suggested this, and another that. ²¹ Finally, a spirit came forward, stood before the LORD and said, 'I will entice him.'

²² "'By what means?' the LORD asked.

"'I will go out and be a lying spirit in the mouths of all his prophets,' he said.

"'You will succeed in enticing him,' said the LORD. 'Go and do it.'

²³ "So now the LORD has put a lying spirit in the mouths of all these prophets of yours. The LORD has decreed disaster for you."

Lesson 10: *Micaiah*

24 Then Zedekiah son of Kenaanah went up and slapped Micaiah in the face. "Which way did the spirit from the LORD go when he went from me to speak to you?" he asked.

25 Micaiah replied, "You will find out on the day you go to hide in an inner room."

26 The king of Israel then ordered, "Take Micaiah and send him back to Amon the ruler of the city and to Joash the king's son **27** and say, 'This is what the king says: Put this fellow in prison and give him nothing but bread and water until I return safely.'"

28 Micaiah declared, "If you ever return safely, the LORD has not spoken through me." Then he added, "Mark my words, all you people!"

A Popular Prophecy (22:1–6)

The events described in our passage took place around 850 B.C., during the time of the divided kingdoms. In prior years, Israel had been at war with Judah and Aram. At this point, Israel and Judah were at peace. Ancient Assyrian sources tell us that Ahab and Israel had been part of a coalition of thirteen kings who challenged Shalmaneser III of Assyria. The Assyrian king was seeking to conquer territories west of the Euphrates River. This coalition successfully repulsed Shalmaneser III at the Battle of Qarqar in 853 B.C. It may have been that relief from the threat of Assyria gave Ahab an opening to seize more territory.

Theologically, Ahab was one of the most wicked Israelite kings, leading his country to new levels of idol worship (see 1 Kings 16:29–33). His Sidonian wife, Jezebel, was instrumental in promoting the worship of her gods (16:31).

After a time of peace between Israel and Aram, Jehoshaphat, king of Judah, went to see Ahab (22:1–3). Jehoshaphat was a righteous king (22:43), but he appears to have been subject to Ahab's authority, perhaps because Judah was weaker than Israel at the time. Although the account doesn't say so, Ahab probably summoned Jehoshaphat to a conference. When he arrived, Ahab reminded him of their mutual claims to Aram and said they needed go to war to attain that area.

Ahab asked Jehoshaphat to join with him in a war of conquest against Aram (22:4–5). Jehoshaphat said all his forces were at Ahab's disposal. Yet the king of Judah wisely made one request to Ahab, that they inquire of the Lord about his will concerning the attack.

Responding to Jehoshaphat's request, Ahab gathered about four hundred prophets of the Lord and asked them whether he and Jehoshaphat should go to war against Aram (22:6). The prophets knew the king wanted to go to war and it was good to please him. So they said he should go, because the Lord was going to deliver Aram into his hands.

Historically, God's leaders and people have often wished to please powerful earthly leaders. This is a universal human desire. Pleasing powerful leaders can avoid pain and bring many earthly rewards. God's leaders and people have also been guilty of mixing patriotism for their country with their faith. They can feel that what's good for their country is good for the kingdom of God and vice-versa. As the story unfolded, these prophets of the Lord were much like those in the German Christian movement, who sought to please power and blend their faith in God with patriotism for their country.

An Unpopular Prophecy (22:7–23)

Jehoshaphat remained hesitant (22:7–9). He sensed this gathering of prophets wasn't revealing God's truth. For this reason, he asked whether there was any other prophet of the Lord of whom they could inquire. Ahab said there was another, but that Ahab hated him because he only prophesied bad things about him. This prophet was Micaiah, son of Imlah. Jehoshaphat gently corrected Ahab for his lack of respect for Micaiah by saying he shouldn't say such a thing about a prophet. Ahab called to one of his officials to bring Micaiah to them.

A dramatic scene followed (22:10–12). The two kings dressed in their beautiful royal robes and sat on their thrones at a threshing floor by the entrance of the main gate of the city of Samaria, the capital of the Northern kingdom. A threshing floor was a large, flat, hard piece of ground on which farmers threshed grain. It provided a large area for the prophetic show that followed. The prophets might have put on a noisy performance, for many of them probably spoke at the same time.

The climax of this display was a symbolic prophecy by Zedekiah, son of Kenaanah. A symbolic prophecy was a dramatic action, sometimes involving physical objects to illustrate the prophecy. People in those times believed that action both expressed the prophecy and assured that the prophecy would come true. Zedekiah made iron horns and said, "This is what the LORD says: 'With these you will gore the Arameans until they are destroyed'" (22:11). All the other prophets joined in saying the same thing.

Meanwhile, the servant whom Ahab sent to summon Micaiah urged the prophet to make it easy on himself by agreeing with the words of the other prophets (22:13–14). Micaiah said he could only say what the Lord told him. When Micaiah arrived, Ahab asked him whether he should go to war against Aram or refrain from doing so. The prophet glibly replied, "Attack . . . and be victorious . . . , for the LORD will give it into the king's hand" (22:14–15).

The king must have sensed sarcasm in the prophet's words, because he demanded Micaiah tell the truth about what the Lord had told him (22:16–17). The prophet did so. He said he saw all Israel scattered across the hills like sheep without a shepherd. In those days, the shepherd was a common image for a king, and so this image meant

Ahab would die. In the prophet's vision, the Lord said, "These people have no master. Let each one go home in peace" (22:17). Ahab would be killed, and his army would scatter and go home in peace.

Ahab responded by turning to Jehoshaphat and saying something like, *There, I told you so! He only prophesies bad things about me!* (see 22:18).

Micaiah continued by telling about a vision the Lord gave him (22:19–23). He saw the Lord seated on his throne with the heavenly host around him. Many ancient people believed that God's divine council surrounded him in heaven, the way an earthly king's advisors, servants, and generals surrounded him. The Lord asked who would entice Ahab to attack the Arameans so he would be killed. Different spirits suggested different possibilities until one said that he would go out and be a lying spirit in the mouths of the prophets. The Lord said he would be successful and he was to go out and do it. The prophet said the Lord put a lying spirit in Ahab's prophets because the Lord had decreed disaster for the king.

We modern Christians may find this vision disturbing because it doesn't fit our view of God and his work. But we need to remember a couple of things. First, it fits how ancient people saw God and life. They believed God directly caused everything to happen, good or bad. While *we* might say God allowed Ahab to go to his death through the lying prophets, *they* would say God put a lying spirit into the prophets. Second, we need to remember the broader point of the vision, which is that God is sovereign over everything. Ahab and Jehoshaphat looked impressive and authoritative sitting on their thrones. But their power was subject to God's power. God's decrees in heaven were what was most important, not their decrees on earth.

The Costliness and Reward of God's Truth (22:24–35)

The assembly didn't appreciate Micaiah's truthful prophecy. Zedekiah was the prophet who dramatically displayed the iron horns as a symbolic prophecy of how Ahab would gore the Arameans. He went up to Micaiah, slapped him in the face, and said, "Which way did the spirit of the Lord go when he went from me to speak to you?" (22:24).

Micaiah responded to this challenge by saying, "You will find out on the day you go to hide in an inner room" (22:25). In other words, Zedekiah would find out when he ran in panic to hide from the coming judgment.

Ahab didn't appreciate Micaiah's prophecy either. He ordered Micaiah confined to the prison and said that he was to receive nothing but bread and water until the king returned safely (22:26–27). Micaiah responded by saying that if Ahab returned safely, the Lord hadn't spoken through him (22:28).

Although Ahab silenced Micaiah, he couldn't stop the word of the Lord. Apparently, Micaiah's prophecy gave

Ahab concern because he disguised himself as he went into battle. He made Jehoshaphat wear his royal robes (22:29–30). The Aramean king ordered his commanders to focus on finding Ahab and killing him (22:31). They spotted Jehoshaphat and pursued him, thinking he was Ahab. But when Jehoshaphat cried out, the commanders saw he wasn't Ahab and turned away from him (22:32–33). In the heat of battle, a random arrow struck Ahab between the sections of his armor. Despite his deception, the king was unable to escape God's judgment. Ahab told his chariot driver to get him out of the battle. The driver did so and propped up Ahab in his chariot, facing the Arameans. The battle raged all day, and the king's blood ran onto the chariot's floor. That evening, Ahab died (22:34–35). As the sun set, word spread throughout the army of the king's death, and the soldiers said, "Every man to his town; everyone to his land!" (22:36).

Despite his best efforts, Ahab couldn't overcome the word of the Lord. Micaiah suffered for his faithfulness to God's revelation, but he experienced the reward of being true to God and seeing his prophecy prevail.

For Life Today

Sometimes speaking God's truth to earthly powers can be painful and dangerous. Believers from Micaiah to the *confessing Christians* of 1930s Germany to prophets of more recent times put their lives in danger by telling authorities things that they didn't want to hear. When there's a great groundswell of public support for going to war or taking away the rights of certain groups, it can be difficult to stand and say that what the group or the power wants to do is contrary to God's word. We want to please earthly powers because they can reward or punish us. The pressure on us can be even greater when the desire of the earthly power matches the desires of the majority of people.

Micaiah's experience reminds us that we can find courage to deliver his word in such circumstances in the knowledge that God, not humans, is in ultimate control of what happens in the world, and that we must ultimately account to him for what we do and say.

THE DIVINE COUNCIL

An important part of Micaiah's prophecy was a vision of God's divine council. In this vision, God deliberated with his council and recruited them to help carry out his will.

Ancient people believed that just as an earthly king surrounded himself with various officials, God in heaven surrounded himself with divine servants. This concept wasn't unique to the Israelites because scholars have found references to it in the literature of Israel's neighbors. Biblical references to this council include Job 1:6, which refers to the members of the council as "the sons of God." The *sons of God* are divine beings who appear to be different from angels. They are divine, but they are less than God and subject to him. Satan, the accuser who challenges God, is a member of this council.

Other references include Psalms 29:1; 82:1; and 89:7. This concept of the divine council may also explain God's use of the words "us" and "our" in Genesis 1:26.

Case Study

A pastor has received a phone call from a church member extending an invitation to a meeting to protest the construction of a mosque in the area. As a traditional Baptist, the pastor believes Baptists ought to support the rights of other faiths to build places of worship. But the pastor knows that refusing to take part in the protest will anger this church member and many others. How should the pastor respond?

QUESTIONS

1. Imagine that you were Micaiah standing before Ahab and Jehoshaphat. What would be your thoughts in that circumstance? What various personal and national interests would come into play? What barriers would you have to overcome to deliver God's word?

2. Think of circumstances when you've had tough choices to make about speaking God's truth. Was it difficult to say what was right? What helped you to speak the truth or stopped you from doing so?

3. What times have arisen in our nation's history in which Christians faced difficulty speaking truth to power? Is it easier to see clearly what is right today than it was in those times? Why or why not?

FOCAL TEXT
2 Chronicles 34:19–31

BACKGROUND
2 Kings 22:1—23:30;
2 Chronicles 34—35

LESSON ELEVEN

Huldah:
Interpreting and Proclaiming God's Message

MAIN IDEA

Huldah, a woman who was a prophet, interpreted and proclaimed God's message.

QUESTION TO EXPLORE

To whom are we willing to listen in order to receive and understand God's message?

STUDY AIM

To describe the role of Huldah in interpreting and proclaiming God's message to Judah's leaders and to state implications for receiving and understanding God's message today

QUICK READ

King Josiah sent messengers to the prophetess Huldah to inquire of the Lord. Huldah said that God would send his judgment on Judah but would spare Josiah.

The role of women in the church has been controversial in Christian denominations and churches in recent decades. Many Christians believe the Bible restricts women from assuming church leadership and from preaching and teaching the Scriptures. Passages like 1 Corinthians 11:3–10 and 1 Timothy 2:11–15 seem to support these restrictions. Some Christians look only at passages like these and don't consider the whole witness of the Bible on this subject. When they do so, they find that what the Bible says about the role of women among God's people is complex. It's true that we find passages that appear to bar women from preaching and teaching, and yet we also find passages that tell of women preaching and teaching with God's apparent blessing. Many Christians are uninformed about this second category of passages.

Many of us know about the great prophets of the Bible, but fewer of us are aware of the prominent prophetesses of the Scriptures. These prophetesses include Miriam (Exodus 15:20), Deborah (Judges 4:4; lesson six), and Huldah, a key figure in our focal text. The Hebrew word *prophetess* is the female form of the word *prophet*. Prophetesses did the same thing that prophets did: deliver the word of the Lord.

As we explore our focal passage, we'll consider the discovery of the word of the Lord in ancient Israel. We'll also think about a word from the Lord delivered by the prophetess Huldah. As we do so, we'll reflect on the question, *To whom are we willing to listen to hear God's message?*

2 Chronicles 34:19–31

19 When the king heard the words of the Law, he tore his robes. **20** He gave these orders to Hilkiah, Ahikam son of Shaphan, Abdon son of Micah, Shaphan the secretary and Asaiah the king's attendant: **21** "Go and inquire of the Lord for me and for the remnant in Israel and Judah about what is written in this book that has been found. Great is the Lord's anger that is poured out on us because our fathers have not kept the word of the Lord; they have not acted in accordance with all that is written in this book."

22 Hilkiah and those the king had sent with him went to speak to the prophetess Huldah, who was the wife of Shallum son of Tokhath, the son of Hasrah, keeper of the wardrobe. She lived in Jerusalem, in the Second District.

23 She said to them, "This is what the Lord, the God of Israel, says: Tell the man who sent you to me, **24** 'This is what the Lord says: I am going to bring disaster on this place and its people—all the curses written in the book that has been read in the presence of the king of Judah. **25** Because they have forsaken me and burned incense to other gods and provoked me to anger by all that their hands have made, my anger will be poured out on this place and will not be quenched.' **26** Tell the king of Judah, who sent you to inquire of the Lord, 'This is what the Lord, the God of Israel, says concerning the words you heard: **27** Because your heart was responsive and you humbled yourself before God when you heard what he spoke against this place and its people, and because you humbled yourself before me and tore your robes and wept in my presence, I have heard you, declares the LORD. ²⁸ Now I will gather you to your fathers, and you will be buried in peace. Your eyes will not see all the disaster I am going to bring on this place and on those who live here.'"

So they took her answer back to the king.

²⁹ Then the king called together all the elders of Judah and Jerusalem. ³⁰ He went up to the temple of the LORD with the men of Judah, the people of Jerusalem, the priests and the Levites—all the people from the least to the greatest. He read in their hearing all the words of the Book of the Covenant, which had been found in the temple of the LORD. ³¹ The king stood by his pillar and renewed the covenant in the presence of the LORD—to follow the LORD and keep his commands, regulations and decrees with all his heart and all his soul, and to obey the words of the covenant written in this book.

Discovery and Reaction (34:1–19)

The events recorded in this lesson's text took place in the late seventh century B.C., around 622. The Assyrians had destroyed the Northern kingdom of Israel in 722 B.C., carrying its inhabitants to other countries and settling people from other lands in its territory. The Southern kingdom of Judah still existed, ruled by King Josiah. Following the assassination of his father Amon, Josiah became king at age eight. Both his father and his grandfather were wicked kings, but Josiah obeyed the Lord and emulated his forefather David. He began a great reform for the Lord in Judah.

The Books of 2 Kings and 2 Chronicles both tell about Josiah and his reform. These books tell basically the same story, but they were written at different times with slightly different points of view. First and Second Kings appear to have been written about the time of the Exile. They start with the latter part of King David's reign and tell about the kings of Israel and Judah. One of their important theological themes is that God sent his people into Exile because of their sins. First and Second Chronicles were written after the Exile. They begin with Adam and tell about Israel's early history through genealogies. They focus on the kings of Judah, and one of their important theological themes is that God still had plans and purposes for his people as they returned to their homeland. We see this difference in their accounts of Josiah's reform, as the account in 2 Kings stresses Israel's sin and coming judgment, while 2 Chronicles stresses the reinstitution of the Passover celebration.

The accounts in 2 Kings and 2 Chronicles are also somewhat different in that 2 Kings suggests that the discovery of the book of the law marked the beginning of Josiah's reform, while 2 Chronicles suggests that the reform was already underway when the book of the law was discovered. That the 2 Kings account says that temple renovation was already underway when the book of the law was discovered suggests that the reform was also underway.

Second Chronicles 34:1–7 tell of Josiah's ascension to the throne and his loyal worship of the Lord. Verses 3–7 speak of his extensive efforts to cleanse his kingdom of idolatry. Verses 8–11 describe how he set out to repair the neglected temple of the Lord in Jerusalem. He raised money from the remnant of the Israelites who lived in the area of the former Northern kingdom and from the people of Judah and Benjamin. Given the descriptions of the extensive work required on the temple, it appears that this once-glorious structure was in a terrible state of disrepair.

While laborers were working on the temple, Hilkiah the priest found the book of the law of the Lord (34:14). Scholars are uncertain about the precise identity of this book. Many believe that it was the Book of Deuteronomy, because of that book's emphasis on a central place of worship. Josiah was committed to destroying all places of worship other than the temple in Jerusalem. Furthermore, the covenant curses recorded in Deuteronomy 28 may explain Josiah's emotional response to the reading of the book.

Hilkiah passed the book of the law on to Shaphan, the king's secretary. When Shaphan went to the king to report on the work of the temple, he said that Hilkiah had given him a book. Shaphan then proceeded to read from it (2 Chron. 34:14–18). When the king heard the words of the book, he tore his robes. Tearing clothes was a common sign of intense grief in those days. It could have been that Hilkiah read these words:

> However, if you do not obey the LORD your God and do not carefully follow all his commands and decrees I am giving you today, all these curses will come upon you and overtake you: You will be cursed in the city and cursed in the country. Your basket and your kneading trough will be cursed. The fruit of your womb will be cursed, and the crops of your land, and the calves of your herds and the lambs of your flocks. You will be cursed when you come in and cursed when you go out. The LORD will send on you curses, confusion and rebuke in everything you put your hand to, until you are destroyed and come to sudden ruin because of the evil you have done in forsaking him (Deuteronomy 28:15–20).

When Josiah heard these words, he knew that he and his people were in great danger of God's judgment.

History is full of stories of great reform movements that began with a rediscovery of the Scriptures. One of the most important of these was the Protestant Reformation. One of the keys to this reformation was the invention of the printing press. Before Johannes Gutenberg invented the printing press in 1436, copies of the Scripture were rare. After the invention of the printing press, many more people were able to read the Bible themselves, resulting in a rediscovery of the Bible. The Reformation, which began in 1517, likely wouldn't have been possible without the printing press.

The Reformers also began to translate the Bible into common languages. For many centuries, only the Latin translation of the Bible was available or allowed. Since most people didn't speak Latin, the common person was unfamiliar with much of the Bible. But as scholars began to translate the Scriptures into languages like German and English, more Christians could understand the Bible. Among the groups benefitting from the printing press and the translation of the Bible into common languages were early Baptists, who believed that all believers should read and interpret the Bible themselves.

In a sense, each generation must rediscover the Bible for itself. We have the constant challenge of removing the *dust* of our rebellion and reading the Scriptures as they are.

A Word from the Lord (34:20–28)

In his state of alarm, Josiah ordered several of his officials to go and inquire of the Lord for him and for the remnant in Israel and Judah about the words written in the book of the law (34:19–21). In those days, the people believed the Lord spoke through prophets. So, when people wanted to learn what God had to say about a matter, they consulted a prophet. In this case, three of Josiah's officials went to consult the prophetess Huldah, who lived in Jerusalem (34:22).

That the three officials went to consult a prophetess may surprise us. Many of us are not accustomed to thinking that a woman can bring a word from the Lord. In fact, some Christians today believe that a woman can't bring a word from the Lord. Yet it appears that Josiah and his officials had no problem consulting a prophetess about what God had to say about their circumstance. Both 2 Kings and 2 Chronicles present this information as a simple matter of fact. Huldah could have been Josiah's court prophetess, supported by the king himself.

Although females overall had low status in the ancient world, it appears that some gifted women rose to extraordinary positions and did extraordinary things. By consulting Huldah, Josiah and his officials showed that God's Spirit filled people regardless of their gender. Given the fact that the Bible refers to prophets much more often than it does to prophetesses, males probably performed this ministry much more often than females. Nonetheless, being a woman wasn't a barrier to bringing a word from the Lord.

The word that Huldah brought from the Lord had two parts: the first concerned the nation, and the second concerned Josiah (34:23–28). She said that all the curses mentioned in the book would fall on the Israelites. They would suffer God's judgment because of their idolatry. Nothing they could do could stop it. Huldah had a less harsh word for Josiah. She said that because he had responded in such grief to the word of the Lord, he wouldn't experience the curses. Instead, he would be buried in peace and not see the disaster that God was bringing.

Curiously, Josiah didn't die a peaceful death. Inexplicably, he engaged King Neco of Egypt in battle. He did this despite the fact that Neco had no intention of attacking him. Josiah was fatally wounded in the battle and buried in Jerusalem (35:20–36). Perhaps the best explanation of the surface discrepancy between Huldah's prophecy and the events that unfolded is that although Josiah died violently, he didn't see his people's destruction and exile. His burial among his fathers was peaceful, although his death wasn't.

For Life Today

This passage suggests at least two lessons for us. First, we need to live in a constant state of spiritual reform. We must revisit the Scriptures every day, and with the guidance of the Holy Spirit measure our lives against God's word. Like the ancient Israelites, we can neglect God's word to such an extent that it nearly becomes forgotten in our lives. We need to make every effort to keep the adulterations of our sins and our culture from obscuring our reading of the Bible.

Second, we need to be careful about saying whom God will and won't use to deliver his word. Many believers today believe that God won't use women to deliver his word, and that if a woman attempts to do so, she's violating scriptural commands. Yet in this passage, Huldah delivered God's message to Josiah without any negative connotation on her spirituality, character, or obedience to God. Furthermore, the word she brought was true. From a scriptural perspective, our main concern should be with the presence of the Holy Spirit in a speaker, not a speaker's gender.

Prophetesses in Scripture

Huldah wasn't alone among the Bible's prophetesses. Miriam, sister of Moses and Aaron, was a prophetess who led Israel in a song about the Lord's victory at the Red Sea (Exod. 15:20). In addition to being a deliverer (judge) of Israel, Deborah was a prophetess who went with her people's army to war (Judges 4). The prophet Isaiah was apparently married to a prophetess (Isaiah 6:3).

Women who brought God's word weren't confined to the Old Testament. Anna, who greeted Joseph, Mary, and Jesus in the temple courts, was a prophetess (Luke

2:36). Phillip the evangelist had four unmarried daughters who prophesied (Acts 21:9). Furthermore, on the day of Pentecost, the Apostle Peter quoted the prophet Joel (Joel 2:28–23), who said that in the last days God would pour out his Spirit on all people, and their sons and daughters would prophesy. He said that this prophecy was fulfilled on that day (Acts 2:16–21).

Most likely, the majority of those who prophesied in the early church were men, but women performed this ministry as well.

Case Study

A young female college student expresses a call to preach during the commitment time in a worship service. Afterwards, a deacon in the church tells her that women are to minister only in the home and to other women.

Dismayed, she comes to you for guidance. What scriptural guidance would you offer her? How would you support her in her calling?

LESSON 11: *Huldah*

QUESTIONS

1. How did the Israelites rediscover the book of the law? Why was Josiah so grieved when he heard the words from it?

2. Why did Josiah send officials to consult with the prophetess Huldah? What was the word of the Lord that she brought?

3. What are our prejudices about whom God will and won't use to bring his word?

4. Think of women who have been spiritually influential in your life. How did God use them?

FOCAL TEXT
Jeremiah 20:7–18; 26:1–15

BACKGROUND
Jeremiah 1:1–10; 20:7–18;
26:1–19; 37:1—38:28

LESSON TWELVE

Jeremiah:
BEING FAITHFUL IN THE DEPTHS OF DESPAIR

MAIN IDEA

The challenges Jeremiah faced in serving God led him to great despair, but he courageously remained faithful.

QUESTION TO EXPLORE

What hard thing is God asking you to do, and how will you respond?

STUDY AIM

To identify implications from Jeremiah's experience for dealing with the challenges I face

QUICK READ

As Jeremiah faithfully proclaimed the message God had called him to deliver, he struggled with despair and discouragement in the face of rebuke, threats, and physical abuse.

In the tough economic times of recent years, many corporations have downsized. In this practice of laying off employees to make the company profitable, middle managers were asked to decide which faithful employees should be given *pink slips.* These managers had then to announce to their friends and co-workers they were no longer employed. Bitterness and resentment were often the result of these conversations, leaving scars on both parties.

Jeremiah found himself in an uncomfortable position. Called by God to be a prophet, Jeremiah had to give Judah a message of gloom and destruction. He found himself ostracized and despised by both leaders and fellow citizens. He sank into deep despair and wondered why he had to be the prophet to deliver such an unpopular message. Yet in the midst of his despair, he remained faithful to God and found God faithful to him.

Jeremiah 20:7–18

⁷ O Lord, you deceived me, and I was deceived;
   you overpowered me and prevailed.
I am ridiculed all day long;
   everyone mocks me.
⁸ Whenever I speak, I cry out
   proclaiming violence and destruction.
So the word of the Lord has brought me
   insult and reproach all day long.

⁹ But if I say, "I will not mention him
  or speak any more in his name,"
his word is in my heart like a fire,
  a fire shut up in my bones.
I am weary of holding it in;
  indeed, I cannot.
¹⁰ I hear many whispering,
  "Terror on every side!
  Report him! Let's report him!"
All my friends
  are waiting for me to slip, saying,
"Perhaps he will be deceived;
  then we will prevail over him
  and take our revenge on him."
¹¹ But the LORD is with me like a mighty warrior;
  so my persecutors will stumble and not prevail.
They will fail and be thoroughly disgraced;
  their dishonor will never be forgotten.
¹² O LORD Almighty, you who examine the righteous
  and probe the heart and mind,
let me see your vengeance upon them,
  for to you I have committed my cause.
¹³ Sing to the LORD!
  Give praise to the LORD!
He rescues the life of the needy
  from the hands of the wicked.
¹⁴ Cursed be the day I was born!
  May the day my mother bore me not be blessed!

¹⁵ Cursed be the man who brought my father the news,
   who made him very glad, saying,
   "A child is born to you—a son!"
¹⁶ May that man be like the towns
   the LORD overthrew without pity.
May he hear wailing in the morning,
   a battle cry at noon.
¹⁷ For he did not kill me in the womb,
   with my mother as my grave,
   her womb enlarged forever.
¹⁸ Why did I ever come out of the womb
   to see trouble and sorrow
   and to end my days in shame?

Jeremiah 26:1–15

¹ Early in the reign of Jehoiakim son of Josiah king of Judah, this word came from the LORD: ² "This is what the LORD says: Stand in the courtyard of the LORD's house and speak to all the people of the towns of Judah who come to worship in the house of the LORD. Tell them everything I command you; do not omit a word. ³ Perhaps they will listen and each will turn from his evil way. Then I will relent and not bring on them the disaster I was planning because of the evil they have done. ⁴ Say to them, 'This is what the LORD says: If you do not listen to me and follow my law, which I have set before you, ⁵ and if you do not listen to the

Lesson 12: *Jeremiah*

words of my servants the prophets, whom I have sent to you again and again (though you have not listened), **6** then I will make this house like Shiloh and this city an object of cursing among all the nations of the earth.'"

7 The priests, the prophets and all the people heard Jeremiah speak these words in the house of the Lord. **8** But as soon as Jeremiah finished telling all the people everything the Lord had commanded him to say, the priests, the prophets and all the people seized him and said, "You must die! **9** Why do you prophesy in the Lord's name that this house will be like Shiloh and this city will be desolate and deserted?" And all the people crowded around Jeremiah in the house of the Lord.

10 When the officials of Judah heard about these things, they went up from the royal palace to the house of the Lord and took their places at the entrance of the New Gate of the Lord's house. **11** Then the priests and the prophets said to the officials and all the people, "This man should be sentenced to death because he has prophesied against this city. You have heard it with your own ears!"

12 Then Jeremiah said to all the officials and all the people: "The Lord sent me to prophesy against this house and this city all the things you have heard. **13** Now reform your ways and your actions and obey the Lord your God. Then the Lord will relent and not bring the disaster he has pronounced against you. **14** As for me, I am in your hands; do with me whatever you think is good and right. **15** Be assured, however, that if you put me to death, you will bring the guilt of innocent blood on yourselves and on this city and on those who live in it, for in truth the Lord has sent me to you to speak all these words in your hearing."

Jeremiah's Call and Context (1:1–10)

Jeremiah began his ministry during Josiah's reign, a bright spot in the bleak, dark decline of the nation of Judah. At the age of eight, Josiah became king in Judah and set his heart on seeking God. In his late teens, he raised money to repair the temple and to rebuild Judean power. During the temple repairs, Hilkiah, the high priest, discovered a book of the law (probably a portion of Deuteronomy). Josiah instituted religious and moral reform, and during this period, Jeremiah experienced his call and began his ministry.

Jeremiah's call is found in chapter 1 and is similar to other calls in the Old Testament. He felt inadequate to speak and attempted to use his youth as an excuse for not being qualified. God reminded him, "Before I formed you in the womb I knew you, before you were born I set you apart" (Jeremiah 1:5). Jeremiah's excuse of being inadequate to speak was answered when the Lord reached out his hand, touched his mouth, and said, "I have put my words in your mouth" (Jer. 1:9). The message he was called to deliver was one "to uproot and tear down, to destroy and overthrow, to build and to plant" (1:10). God did promise, as he did to every servant of his, "I am with you" (1:19).

With the reform of Josiah, Jeremiah's early ministry met with a degree of acceptance. Chapters 2—6 are most likely the messages of the sensitive, courageous young prophet, who, called by Yahweh, wanted to see the nation return to the covenant relationship with its God. With the tragic, untimely death of the king in 609 B.C., the nation slid back into moral, political, and religious decay. The people and leaders no longer looked upon the messages of repentance and reform with favor and began criticizing the prophet.

Jeremiah's Complaint (20:7–18)

Jeremiah had just proclaimed a message pronouncing God's judgment on the people because "they were stiff-necked and would not listen to my words" (19:15). Pashur, a chief officer of the temple, heard the message and had Jeremiah beaten and placed in stocks overnight. Upon his release, Jeremiah reiterated the prophecy of Judah's destruction and declared the personal demise of Pashur and his family (20:1–6). As Jeremiah reflected on what had happened, he reached the lowest point in his ministry and poured out his despair and discouragement to God.

Jeremiah began his complaint by questioning God's call. He felt "deceived" and "overpowered." The words almost sound blasphemous, and at first glance, one is appalled at the accusation. Jeremiah appeared to accuse God of trickery and forcing him to do his bidding. While the words appear to be harsh, they are the words of a servant who is discouraged and doubting whether he is the right person for the job. God had not promised him an easy task. God had told him "the kings of Judah, its officials, its priests and the people of the land . . . will fight against you" (1:18–19). God, however, promised Jeremiah they "will not overcome you, for I am with you and will rescue you" (1:19).

The prophet was frustrated with the unresponsiveness of those he was trying to call back to God. The message of "violence and destruction" was "the word of the Lord" (20:8), but all it had brought was ridicule, mockery, insult, and reproach. I know many pastors and staff members who share Jeremiah's frustration, *Why am I doing this? No one seems to care. All I ever get are people who tell me I am too harsh in my messages. Why did you call ME to this work?* God's true servants develop such a dependency upon him they can bear their heart to him without fear of reproach.

The moment the prophet decided to cease speaking, he realized the message was "in my heart like a fire, a fire shut up in my bones" (20:9). What a marvelous picture of the effect of the word of God. We have watched in horror as wild fires in the Western regions of our country burn, destroying houses and countless acres of forest.

The myriad of techniques and manpower used to try to control these fires is astounding. Just as the fire seems to be contained or extinguished, suddenly the wind shifts. Jeremiah might have wished he could be silent, but he could not contain the message God had placed in his heart.

Jeremiah reminded himself God was "like a mighty warrior," and his enemies would "stumble . . . not prevail . . . fail . . . and be thoroughly disgraced" (20:11–12). God knew Jeremiah's heart, and he understood the commitment of the prophet to the task set before him. Jeremiah suddenly broke into song and praise of the Lord, echoing the promise God had made to rescue him from those who sought to do him harm.

Had the narrative ended with verse 13, we would have thought Jeremiah had worked through his depression and despair. But it had worsened. Verses 14–18 pose a bit of a problem for commentators who struggle with the position of these verses. Some want to suggest they are out of order, and others simply say this is a different instance, not the same one. While we may not be able to resolve this issue, we are allowed to witness the true depth of the depression of the man of God. Jeremiah was overwhelmed with the situation into which he had been called, and we see his struggle in his wishing he had not even been born.

In this depth of despair, Jeremiah wished he had died in his mother's womb. Had he been stillborn, he would not have had to live through the "trouble and sorrow and to end my days in shame" (20:18). While the prophet clamored for his own demise, he clung to his calling, realizing his worth was found in his faithful following of this clarion call of the Lord.

As believers in the risen Lord, our calling is just as clear to proclaim the new life found in Christ. That message is not popular in a world saturated with self-indulgence and focused on feeling good about oneself. As Christ's followers, we are called to deliver a grace-filled message to an ungrateful people who are alienated from God—very much like the prophet.

Jeremiah's Confrontation (26:1–15)

Chapter 26 is known as the temple sermon and is linked to chapters 7—10. This sermon was preached during the reign of Jehoiakim after the death of Josiah and the capture and imprisonment of Jehoahaz by Pharaoh Neco. Jehoiakim was nothing more than a puppet king under Pharaoh's control. We find here a condensed version of the sermon.

Jeremiah spoke to all the assembled—"the priests, the prophets, and all the people." His message again reminded them of their stubbornness to listen to the words of God's prophets and to follow the law. He announced two horrifying results of their sin. The temple would be destroyed like the one in Shiloh. This was a reference to the capture of the ark of the covenant by the Philistines, the death of Eli and his sons, and the dismantling of the tabernacle, which had housed the ark during the reign of Saul.

People of the time believed the temple in Jerusalem was a symbol of God's presence. As long as the temple was present, they had nothing to fear, for God would protect his people regardless how disobedient and wayward they might become. One of the key phrases Jeremiah used in the sermon was, "Peace, peace . . . , when there is no peace" (6:14; 8:11).

Jeremiah further incurred their wrath by pronouncing the city of Jerusalem would become "an object of cursing among all the nations of the earth" (26:6). This struck at the heart of the covenant of God with his people. From the very beginning of his agreement with Abraham to Jeremiah's day, God's desire was for his people to demonstrate his glory to the nations so through them the nations would be blessed. Because of their rejection and idolatry, Jeremiah pronounced their destruction and their becoming a curse in the eyes of the nations.

The message drew an immediate response from those present. They seized him and called for his death because they believed he had blasphemed the temple and the city. The political leaders were immediately made aware of the situation either by messenger or the tumult that had erupted in the temple. They made their way quickly to the temple area and set up court. Jeremiah's captors immediately called for his death based on his treasonous statement—"he has prophesied against this city" (26:11). Jeremiah reiterated the Lord's prophecy against the temple and the city, calling again for the hearers to reform "your ways and your actions and obey the Lord your God" (26:13). He assured them if they did reform, "the LORD would relent and not bring the disaster" (26:13).

The prophet responded, "As for me, I am in your hands, do with me whatever you think is good and right" (26:14). He warned that should they choose to put him to death, they would be shedding "innocent blood . . . for in truth the LORD has sent me to you to speak all these words" (26:15). Jeremiah not only demonstrated his faithfulness in delivering the message, but he also spoke as one who had come to grips with the reality of his confidence in the One who had called him. Regardless of the outcome, Jeremiah was faithful to God, knowing God would be faithful to him.

This Lesson and Life

Many of us struggle with discouragement in our spiritual life, although probably not to the extent of Jeremiah. We may become frustrated with our fickleness in attempting to be consistent with our personal quiet time and prayer life. As we mature, we often find it difficult to balance all the activities of our lives and continue to keep Christ and the call to discipleship in the proper place. As the Holy Spirit begins to prompt us to share our witness with others, we find our hearts broken by those unaware of their lostness and indifference to the grace God has offered.

It would be much easier if we could just live our lives in some cloistered community without ever dealing with a lost, irreligious world. Our only hope for a real relationship with our Lord is found in knowing we are being faithful and doing what he has us called to do.

WORD STUDY

The use of "deceived" and "overpowered" (20:7) to describe how God had called Jeremiah no doubt appears to many readers as harsh and borders on blasphemy. A further study of these words reveals these meanings are a bit more tempered than our understanding. The root idea of "deceived" is *to open,* or *to make roomy.* The word could be translated *allure, entice,* or *persuade.* God does not use deception to call his servants, but he does open their eyes and hearts to see the potential their serving will bring to his kingdom. Jeremiah saw the opportunity to serve and bring about renewal of God's people.

The word "overpowered" has a root idea of *to be able.* The word can also be translated *prevail or endure*, and may be more understood to refer to how God addressed the excuses of Jeremiah. God had an answer for every reason Jeremiah gave for not being worthy of serving. God had prevailed in his call of Jeremiah.

Personal Preparation for Discouragement

To prepare and gain strength for times of discouragement:

- Develop a prayer life where you talk to God about what you feel, not just about what you need
- Spend time on a daily basis reading and understanding God's word
- Be diligent in your service to the Lord and his church, knowing that sometimes your actions will be misunderstood
- Read the biographies of faithful Christians, and note how each dealt with discouragement and disappointment

QUESTIONS

1. Why do you think Jeremiah poured out his heart as he did to God? Was he justified in his depth of depression?

2. How does your understanding of these passages affect your perception of Jeremiah as one of the great prophets of God? Has it increased or decreased? Why?

3. Have you ever experienced something that plunged you into the sort of despair Jeremiah had? How did you recover?

4. Do you serve in an organization where your values are challenged? Do you speak up, or do you compromise? If you speak up, how are you perceived by those with opposite views?

FOCAL TEXT
Daniel 3

BACKGROUND
Daniel 1—3

LESSON THIRTEEN

Shadrach, Meshach, and Abednego:
Giving Unlimited Devotion to God

MAIN IDEA

Shadrach, Meshach, and Abednego vowed to give their full devotion to their God even if they perished.

QUESTION TO EXPLORE

What level of risk is worthwhile in expressing devotion to God?

STUDY AIM

To summarize the story of Shadrach, Meshach, and Abednego and to consider the lengths to which I would go in expressing devotion to God

QUICK READ

When faced with the demand to bow down and worship a pagan image, Shadrach, Meshach, and Abednego refused and remained faithful to God even in the face of death.

Few if any of us have ever been subjected to any sort of severe persecution as a result of our religious beliefs. Yet throughout our world, people are persecuted and, in some extreme instances, executed for their faith in the Lord Jesus Christ.

Our lesson this week is one of the most recounted stories of the Old Testament. It is the story of three Hebrew young men whose faith was tested. When instructed to bow down to an image of a false god, they refused and found themselves facing death. Even in the face of their own death, they determined not to compromise their faith in God. What was meant to bring them harm became the source for praise and brought glory to God.

Daniel 3

¹ King Nebuchadnezzar made an image of gold, ninety feet high and nine feet wide, and set it up on the plain of Dura in the province of Babylon. ² He then summoned the satraps, prefects, governors, advisers, treasurers, judges, magistrates and all the other provincial officials to come to the dedication of the image he had set up. ³ So the satraps, prefects, governors, advisers, treasurers, judges, magistrates and all the other provincial officials assembled for the dedication of the image that King Nebuchadnezzar had set up, and they stood before it.

4 Then the herald loudly proclaimed, "This is what you are commanded to do, O peoples, nations and men of every language: **5** As soon as you hear the sound of the horn, flute, zither, lyre, harp, pipes and all kinds of music, you must fall down and worship the image of gold that King Nebuchadnezzar has set up. **6** Whoever does not fall down and worship will immediately be thrown into a blazing furnace."

7 Therefore, as soon as they heard the sound of the horn, flute, zither, lyre, harp and all kinds of music, all the peoples, nations and men of every language fell down and worshiped the image of gold that King Nebuchadnezzar had set up.

8 At this time some astrologers came forward and denounced the Jews. **9** They said to King Nebuchadnezzar, "O king, live forever! **10** You have issued a decree, O king, that everyone who hears the sound of the horn, flute, zither, lyre, harp, pipes and all kinds of music must fall down and worship the image of gold, **11** and that whoever does not fall down and worship will be thrown into a blazing furnace. **12** But there are some Jews whom you have set over the affairs of the province of Babylon—Shadrach, Meshach and Abednego—who pay no attention to you, O king. They neither serve your gods nor worship the image of gold you have set up."

13 Furious with rage, Nebuchadnezzar summoned Shadrach, Meshach and Abednego. So these men were brought before the king, **14** and Nebuchadnezzar said to them, "Is it true, Shadrach, Meshach and Abednego, that you do not serve my gods or worship the image of gold I have set up? **15** Now when you hear the sound of the horn, flute, zither, lyre, harp, pipes and all kinds of music, if you are ready to fall down and worship the image I made, very good. But if you do not worship it, you will be thrown immediately into a blazing furnace. Then what god will be able to rescue you from my hand?"

16 Shadrach, Meshach and Abednego replied to the king, "O Nebuchadnezzar, we do not need to defend ourselves before you in this matter. **17** If we are thrown into the blazing furnace, the God we serve is able to save us from it, and he will rescue us from your hand, O king. **18** But even if he does not, we want you to know, O king, that we will not serve your gods or worship the image of gold you have set up."

19 Then Nebuchadnezzar was furious with Shadrach, Meshach and Abednego, and his attitude toward them changed. He ordered the furnace heated seven times hotter than usual **20** and commanded some of the strongest soldiers in his army to tie up Shadrach, Meshach and Abednego and throw them into the blazing furnace. **21** So these men, wearing their robes, trousers, turbans and other clothes, were bound and thrown into the blazing furnace. **22** The king's command was so urgent and the furnace so hot that the flames of the fire killed the soldiers who took up Shadrach, Meshach and Abednego, **23** and these three men, firmly tied, fell into the blazing furnace.

24 Then King Nebuchadnezzar leaped to his feet in amazement and asked his advisers, "Weren't there three men that we tied up and threw into the fire?"

They replied, "Certainly, O king."

25 He said, "Look! I see four men walking around in the fire, unbound and unharmed, and the fourth looks like a son of the gods."

26 Nebuchadnezzar then approached the opening of the blazing furnace and shouted, "Shadrach, Meshach and Abednego, servants of the Most High God, come out! Come here!"

So Shadrach, Meshach and Abednego came out of the fire, **27** and the satraps, prefects, governors and royal advisers crowded around them. They saw that the fire had not harmed their bodies, nor was a hair of their heads singed; their robes were not scorched, and there was no smell of fire on them.

28 Then Nebuchadnezzar said, "Praise be to the God of Shadrach, Meshach and Abednego, who has sent his angel and rescued his servants! They trusted in him and defied the king's command and were willing to give up their lives rather than serve or worship any god except their own God. **29** Therefore I decree that the people of any nation or language who say anything against the God of Shadrach, Meshach and Abednego be cut into pieces and their houses be turned into piles of rubble, for no other god can save in this way."

30 Then the king promoted Shadrach, Meshach and Abednego in the province of Babylon.

Nebuchadnezzar's Demand (3:1–7)

Nebuchadnezzar first besieged Jerusalem "in the third year of the reign of Jehoiakim" (Daniel 1:1), about 606 B.C. Following Nebuchadnezzar's defeat of Jerusalem, he took as the spoils of victory the king, some of the articles of the temple, and some of the "royal family and the nobility—young men without any physical defect, handsome, showing aptitude for every kind of learning, well informed, quick to understand, and qualified to serve in the king's palace" (Dan. 1:4). Daniel, Hananiah, Mishael, and Azariah were among those led off in captivity. They were given the Babylonian names of Belteshazzar, Shadrach, Meshach, and Abednego.

While being trained to serve in the Babylonian palace, the four young men refused to eat the lavish, opulent food that was served in the palace and requested to be fed only vegetables and water. After proving to their captors that their diet made them healthier, they also demonstrated to be better "in every matter of wisdom and understanding about which the king questioned them" (1:20) and were chosen for the king's service.

Several years later, Nebuchadnezzar made an image of gold some ninety feet high and nine feet wide. The image was probably not solid gold but was constructed from some other material and overlaid in gold. It might have been erected to celebrate the complete destruction of the city of Jerusalem and Judah (possibly 587 B.C.) and may have been prompted by the interpretation of the king's dream by Daniel in chapter 2. Whether the image was of the king himself or a deity of his nation is not clear, but it was clearly to be an object of worship.

The king summoned all the national leaders to come to the dedication of the image. When all were assembled, Nebuchadnezzar's demand was proclaimed. He commanded that when they heard the sound of the musical instruments, everyone was to "fall down and worship the image of gold" (3:5). Anyone who chose not to abide by the king's directive would "immediately be thrown into a blazing furnace" (3:6).

The image was erected "on the plain of Dura in the province of Babylon" (3:1). It is not clear where this was geographically, but by the attendance it evidently must have been near the city. When the music sounded, "all the peoples, nations and men of every language fell down and worshiped the image of gold" (3:7). Imagine the scene— thousands of people falling prostrate to worship a giant image of gold at a certain sound from some musical instruments.

Why would people do something like this? Many had watched as this mammoth image was constructed and knew it was of no unusual origin. Yet, as the music sounded they complied with the king's decree. Two reasons immediately come to mind for such behavior. First and foremost is fear—fear of the ruthless, powerful leader who issued the command. They knew all too well his ability to carry out his promise of punishment. Many, while fearful, were also wishing to incur the favor of the king and wished to be seen complying with his wishes. Most of us know people who will do whatever it takes to curry the favor of their superior for their own self-promotion.

Shadrach, Meshach, and Abednego's Defiance and Deliverance (3:8–23)

The rise of three Israelites to places of prominence in the palace of King Nebuchadnezzar had not gone unnoticed by their peers. "Some astrologers" (3:8), possibly Chaldeans, felt the duty to inform the king that the Israelites did not bow down at the ceremony that day. The king needed to know these men "whom you have set over the affairs of the province . . . pay no attention to you" (3:12). Not only did they not bow down, but they also "neither serve your gods nor worship the image of gold you have set up" (3:12).

The accusers acted out of jealousy and probably felt their report would garner them some special recognition. Whether it did or did not is of no consequence; the accusation immediately drew the anger of Nebuchadnezzar, who summoned Shadrach, Meshach, and Abednego. His question was clear, "Is it true . . . , that you do not serve my gods or worship the image of gold I have set up?" (3:14). Although there is little question of his anger, the king couched his remarks in a way that allowed for the young men to have a reprieve if they would agree to bow down when the music sounded the next time. He assured them of their punishment if they refused. He remarked, "What god will be able to rescue you from my hand?" (3:15).

Shadrach, Meshach, and Abednego responded by telling the king, "we do not need to defend ourselves before you in this matter" (3:16). They informed the king their God was able to save them from the blazing furnace and indeed could rescue them from the king. They affirmed their trust of God, "But even if he does not, we want you to know, O king, that we will not serve your gods or worship the image of gold you have set up" (3:18). This statement demonstrated their faith more significantly than the initial defiance of the edict. Shadrach, Meshach, and Abednego were saying they trusted their God in whatever decision he made concerning their lives. They trusted him completely.

Some skeptics would point to this as fatalism—simply whatever happens will happen. This was not the belief of these young men. They believed their God would rescue them from the king. They knew God could preserve them through the flame but also believed he would do for them what was best, which might mean their death. They wanted the king to know that no matter what plan God had for them, his plan was better than serving Nebuchadnezzar. Rather than fatalism, this was the belief in a divine design for their lives that they knew was of God.

The text suggests Nebuchadnezzar might have had some sort of admiration for these young men. However, their defiance further infuriated him, and "his attitude toward them changed." He had the furnace heated "seven times hotter than usual" (3:19), which probably means it was heated to the highest temperature possible. Designed for making bricks, the furnace would now be used as a method of destruction of human lives. Shadrach, Meshach, and Abednego were bound still wearing their ceremonial garments and thrown into the furnace by the king's "strongest soldiers," (3:20), who were consumed by the flames and the intense heat of the furnace.

When the flames died down, Nebuchadnezzar "leaped to his feet in amazement" (3:24), asking for confirmation of the number of those thrown into the fire. His advisers assured him there had been three, but he ordered them to gaze into the flames and to "see four men walking around in the fire, unbound and unharmed, and the fourth looks like a son of the gods" (3:25).

The identity of the fourth person in the fiery furnace is always a matter of dispute. Whether this was an angel, a pre-incarnation appearance of Christ, or some other sort of theophany does not appear to have been important to Nebuchadnezzar. He realized the God of Shadrach, Meshach, and Abednego had demonstrated his ability to protect and deliver his servants from the fiery furnace.

The king immediately called to the young men to come out of the furnace. He called them by their names and referred to them as "the servants of the Most High God" (3:26). An audience gathered as the three men came out of the furnace. They were all amazed. Shadrach, Meshach, and Abednego were unharmed by the fire. Their clothes were not scorched, there was no smell of smoke, and not a hair on them was singed. Their God had proven beyond any measurable means to be greater than the gods of Nebuchadnezzar.

Nebuchadnezzar's Decree (3:24–30)

Just as his attitude had changed in anger toward the young men's defiance, Nebuchadnezzar now had a completely different attitude toward the God of Shadrach, Meshach, and Abednego. He admitted their God had been able to save them as "no other god can save" (3:29), and their trust in him was neither misplaced nor misguided.

King Nebuchadnezzar decreed not to say anything against the God of Shadrach, Meshach, or Abednego. He further declared that anyone who did speak against their God would "be cut into pieces and their houses be turned into piles of rubble" (3:29). His final act was to promote Shadrach, Meshach, and Abednego to new positions in Babylon.

What a day it had been! Thousands worshiped an idol at the king's whim, but three young men stood in opposition to the Babylonian monarch's decree. Thrown into a fiery furnace, Shadrach, Meshach, and Abednego stood unscathed by the flames and unshaken by the monarch's threat. On that day it was not a golden image that received honor, but the God of Shadrach, Meshach, and Abednego that received the faithful obedience of his servants and the acknowledgment of honor and praise by the king of Babylon.

This Lesson and Life

Few of us will ever face the sort of persecution the three Israelite young men faced, but we will be challenged concerning our faith. We may be challenged to participate in activities that compromise our beliefs. Suddenly we find ourselves being looked upon as narrow-minded prudes.

In the business world in recent years, we have witnessed men and women who have compromised their values in order to profit themselves. In doing this, other men and women have had to step forward and become whistleblowers on the unethical behavior of others. Many times these individuals were looked upon with disdain, and some have found it difficult to continue in their company and even in their chosen vocation.

Likely you have been challenged at some point in your life to take a stand for what you believe is right. Whether you were lauded and applauded or cursed and condemned, you can know that you have pleased your Lord when you have been faithful. That feeling of bringing honor and praise to him is what truly matters.

Word Study

Idioms are found in the Hebrew language as in our own. An idiom is the use of words that when grouped together suggest something different from their combined meanings, such as a phrase like *put an extra pair of eyes* on something or *beat a dead horse.* In Daniel 3:8 the astrologers "denounced" Shadrach, Meshach, and Abednego. The word used in the verse is actually two Hebrew words that form an idiomatic phrase. Both Hebrew words have root ideas of *eat* or *devour*, and one of the words has the idea of *chewing the pieces or morsels.* We might say in English the astrologers were *chewing them up and spitting them out.* This was an act of malicious intent. The accusers were intent on destroying the Hebrews and were doing so with fervor. There can be little doubt these Chaldeans were jealous and wanted to tip the scales in their own favor at the expense of Shadrach, Meshach, and Abednego.

Become Aware

Become more aware of the worldwide persecution of Christian both individually and corporately by spending a few minutes on the internet and exploring sites that document such persecution. Sites such as *Voice of the Martyrs* (www.persecution.com) and *Christian Persecution Magazine* (www.christianpersecution.info) regularly update details on persecution. These sites also suggest ways you can become involved through promoting awareness and prayer for those being persecuted.[1]

QUESTIONS

1. How do you think the accusers of Shadrach, Meshach, and Abednego felt about what happened to them ultimately?

2. Why do you think Nebuchadnezzar referred to God as the God of Shadrach, Meshach, and Abednego and not as the God of Israel?

3. In what area of your life have you been challenged to compromise your faith?

4. What can you do to prepare yourself for the challenges of compromising your beliefs and faith? How will you help others (family or friends) in this area?

NOTES

1. Sites accessed 1/6/2011.

FOCAL TEXT
Esther 4:1–16

BACKGROUND
Esther 1—8

LESSON FOURTEEN

Esther:
Taking the Ultimate Risk

MAIN IDEA

Esther's risking her life for an uncertain outcome enabled her people to escape death.

QUESTION TO EXPLORE

What level of risk is worthwhile in extending help to people?

STUDY AIM

To summarize the story of Esther and consider the lengths to which I would go in extending help to people

QUICK READ

Although Esther had no voice and no choice within her cultural context, her faith in God impacted the lives and history of her people.

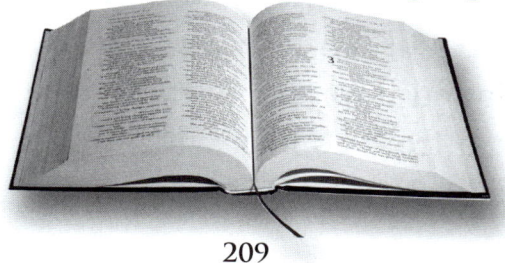

Everyone who flies knows that bad weather can cause problems with air travel. Recently my parents landed in one flight only to discover that their connecting flight had been cancelled due to storms in the vicinity of their next stop. Instead of changing planes for a quick trip home, many travelers, like my parents, found themselves grounded for the night.

Some events in life veer beyond our control. A natural disaster or catastrophic illness, for example, may leave the victims feeling helpless, vulnerable, or frightened. Esther probably experienced similar emotions when she was singled out for the king's harem.

In ancient Persian society, a concubine was a low-ranking wife who brought no dowry or political connections into a marriage. The large number of girls in a royal harem limited the number and frequency of individual visits with the king. Most would never see him again after their initial visit to his bedchamber. If that union resulted in pregnancy, the child might be raised to serve in a high government position but would never be considered an heir in the royal bloodline. That right fell only to sons produced by the queen. Although concubines were pampered with clothes, servants, and richly-adorned apartments, they had no chance for normal lives with husbands, children, or private homes, and were never allowed to return to their own families. They were isolated from contact with people outside the palace, like pet birds in a cage.

For innocent teenage girls like Esther, the prospect of life as a king's concubine would seem the equivalent of a prison sentence. When she was gathered into a group of virgins destined for the harem, she had no say in the matter and no choice but to obey the summons or forfeit her life. She was a helpless victim in circumstances beyond her control.

ESTHER 4:1–16

¹ When Mordecai learned of all that had been done, he tore his clothes, put on sackcloth and ashes, and went out into the city, wailing loudly and bitterly. ² But he went only as far as the king's gate, because no one clothed in sackcloth was allowed to enter it. ³ In every province to which the edict and order of the king came, there was great mourning among the Jews, with fasting, weeping and wailing. Many lay in sackcloth and ashes.

⁴ When Esther's maids and eunuchs came and told her about Mordecai, she was in great distress. She sent clothes for him to put on instead of his sackcloth, but he would not accept them. ⁵ Then Esther summoned Hathach, one of the king's eunuchs assigned to attend her, and ordered him to find out what was troubling Mordecai and why.

⁶ So Hathach went out to Mordecai in the open square of the city in front of the king's gate. ⁷ Mordecai told him everything that had happened to him, including the exact

amount of money Haman had promised to pay into the royal treasury for the destruction of the Jews. **8** He also gave him a copy of the text of the edict for their annihilation, which had been published in Susa, to show to Esther and explain it to her, and he told him to urge her to go into the king's presence to beg for mercy and plead with him for her people.

9 Hathach went back and reported to Esther what Mordecai had said. **10** Then she instructed him to say to Mordecai, **11** "All the king's officials and the people of the royal provinces know that for any man or woman who approaches the king in the inner court without being summoned the king has but one law: that he be put to death. The only exception to this is for the king to extend the gold scepter to him and spare his life. But thirty days have passed since I was called to go to the king."

12 When Esther's words were reported to Mordecai, **13** he sent back this answer: "Do not think that because you are in the king's house you alone of all the Jews will escape. **14** For if you remain silent at this time, relief and deliverance for the Jews will arise from another place, but you and your father's family will perish. And who knows but that you have come to royal position for such a time as this?"

15 Then Esther sent this reply to Mordecai: **16** "Go, gather together all the Jews who are in Susa, and fast for me. Do not eat or drink for three days, night or day. I and my maids will fast as you do. When this is done, I will go to the king, even though it is against the law. And if I perish, I perish."

Privilege Without Freedom (4:1–8)

The king in Esther's story is Xerxes I (called Ahasuerus in Hebrew), a Persian emperor who reigned around 485–464 B.C. Some time after his official wife Vashti lost favor, Xerxes decided to replace her. His attendants initiated a search for the most beautiful young women in the kingdom. After a year of extensive beauty treatments, being continually lathered with rich oils and perfumes, each of these virgins spent a night in the king's bed. The one who pleased him most became the new queen. As it turned out, Esther won this problematic competition.

Some girls may have enjoyed the luxury of palace life. With an army of servants at their disposal, they ate the best foods and enjoyed fine clothes and jewelry. But the situation created a difficult predicament for Esther. Her Jewish faith bound her to a much stricter moral code than that of her pagan counterparts. She was forced to sleep with a Gentile man who was not her husband, and then further to violate Jewish law by marrying him (Deuteronomy 7:3). Jewish commentators throughout history have either excused her behavior, considering her night with the king a case of forcible rape, or condemned her choice to deny her faith and save her life through immoral actions.[1] No matter the interpretations of outsiders, Esther's dilemma was difficult and confusing. Through no fault of her own, she was plunged into a situation that deprived her of freedom and personal honor. As queen, she enjoyed a high level of prestige within the royal court, but she maintained it only by hiding her true ethnic and religious identity and conforming to political protocol. In reality, Esther was no more than a pampered prisoner.

The person Esther looked to for guidance in these circumstances was Mordecai, a cousin who had adopted and raised her after her parents died. He advised the new queen to conceal her Jewish roots. Mordecai was an upright man, but his sense of honor bought him an enemy when he refused to bow down and pay respect to Haman, one of the king's top officials. Unlike Esther, Mordecai openly acknowledged his Jewish heritage. Haman's anger toward Mordecai festered until it exploded into hatred for the entire Jewish race. Taking advantage of his high position and the king's trust, Haman plotted to exterminate all the Jews in the empire by convincing Xerxes to sign an irrevocable death warrant against them. But Mordecai also had connections in the court. He turned to the queen for help, reminding Esther that an edict against the Jews threatened her life as well as theirs.

A Perilous Predicament (4:9–11)

Esther was caught in a difficult situation. Mordecai wanted her to take advantage of her favor with the king and asked Esther to petition the king for mercy on behalf of her people. But his request presented a danger for the queen herself. Anyone who approached the king without being summoned by him was put to death unless he intervened with a pardon. Xerxes had not sent for his wife in a month. If Esther tried to see the king without permission, she might die by his command. But if she did nothing, she might die along with the other Jews on the day of mass execution. Either option put her life at risk. Once more she became a victim of circumstances beyond her control.

The Hand of God (4:12–14)

When leaders of the early church were considering which writings should be included in the Christian Bible, the Book of Esther was hotly debated because God's name does not appear in it. The omission of God's name, though, does not mean that God is absent from the story. On the contrary, God's presence, activity, and power are evident throughout the entire book. Consider Mordecai's response to Esther's protests. His assertion in verse 14 that "relief and deliverance for the Jews will arise" was a reference to God's care and provision for his chosen people. He also believed that Esther's failure to act would result in God's punishment ("you and your father's family will perish"). And nowhere in Scripture is found a more poignant reminder of God's sovereign will than in the words, "who knows but that you have come to royal position for such a time as this?" (Esther 4:14). In this statement Mordecai acknowledged God's plan as the framework within which all circumstances and events are governed. On a more personal level, perhaps it also absolved Esther of any guilt associated with her rise to rank, since it was God's design that put her there.

God's deliverance emerges as a central theme in this passage. Jews living in exile under Persian rule would be able to draw parallels between their own captivity and the oppression Israel experienced during Egyptian enslavement. Just as God used Moses' royal education and years of wilderness shepherding to prepare him for leadership, so he used Esther's unique position to influence the course of history. Although Esther's journey was marked with humiliation and heartbreak, God worked in her circumstances to bring her heart to obedience, as he had with Moses. In both stories, God revealed himself as a God who wastes nothing but involves himself in the lives of both individuals and nations to accomplish his plan.

Faith in Action (4:15–16)

Esther's call for a national fast emphasized the importance of corporate prayer. Fasting would lead the Jews to humble themselves and purify their hearts before presenting a request to God. Although living as expatriates in a foreign land, the whole nation would be united in prayer and petition.

In verse 16, Esther responded to her people's need by laying aside any concerns for her personal safety. With a selflessness that foreshadowed New Testament precepts (see Philippians 2:3–8), she allowed their interests to take precedent over her own. Her declaration of intent to approach the king, under threat of death, telegraphed a spiritual climax that peaked in total surrender. The words "if I perish, I perish" represent Esther's acknowledgment of and complete submission to God's sovereignty over her life (4:16). No matter the degree to which Esther felt willing to help others, her private inclinations became subordinate to God's call. She responded to the impulse of his divine will.

Only when Esther released her life into God's Lordship was he able to use her for his purpose. She did risk death by approaching the king, who in turn spared her life. She did exercise patience and restraint, introducing the subject of Jewish martyrdom when the king was most receptive instead of abruptly blurting it out in an emotional frenzy. The edict inciting national massacre of Jews could not be rescinded, but Xerxes accepted Esther's suggestion that her people be allowed to fight back. Rather than becoming an anti-Semitic holocaust, the day turned into a sweeping victory for the Jews.

Now, more than 2,000 years later, the Jewish people still celebrate this story of God's deliverance from Persian persecution. The feast of Purim is an annual two-day celebration that takes place during the month of Adar on the Jewish calendar (usually falling sometime around March). Esther 9:22 describes it as a commemoration of "the time when the Jews got relief from their enemies, and as the month when their sorrow was tuned into joy and their mourning into a day of celebration." The holiday's name itself stems from the Persian word *pur*, which is the lot or die that Haman cast to determine the day of his intended Jewish massacre. Although Purim is not one of the feasts commanded by the Law of Moses, it is celebrated as a reminder of God's faithfulness to his covenant people. As the heroine of the story, Esther is not applauded for her beauty or courage so much as she is held up as an example of self-sacrifice and trust in God.

This Lesson and Life

In Esther's cultural and historical context, she had few personal rights or freedoms. Her society allowed her no voice in determining the events of her life. Yet she made a difference in her world. Her choice to trust God in difficult circumstances had an impact on the history of her entire nation.

We may not think that our sphere of influence is very large, or that our personal choices make much difference to people around us. But we never know how God may use our words, actions, or attitudes to influence others. A gesture that seems small to us may have significant impact on another person's response to God. If we follow Christ, every area of our lives should reflect his attributes. We are to perceive and evaluate everything from the lens of his eternal perspective. That means we will pattern our choices and decisions after his, instead of clinging to our own impulses and desires. Just as Esther became willing to lay aside her own interests for the sake of others, we should learn to release all concerns to God's sovereign care. Seeing our obedience may be a pivotal factor in another person's move toward faith.

Acts of Mourning or Repentance

In the ancient world, people of many cultures shared a custom of sprinkling dirt or ashes on their heads as a sign of mourning. Tearing the clothes and smearing dust on the head and body was a symbolic identification with the decay of death and burial (see Genesis 37:34–35). New Testament writers would later associate the practice with repentance of sin (see Matthew 11:21).

Sackcloth was a coarse fabric usually made of goat or camel hair. Sometimes worn by prophets as a form of self-denial (see Matt. 3:4), sackcloth was most often used in connection with funerary mourning practices. At times, people who had experienced a great injustice would wear sackcloth as an expression of their grief and distress. During the period of Persia's dominance, it was common to see these individuals standing and wailing outside the king's gate, hoping to call his attention to their plight, but usually such people would not be allowed inside the palace complex.

Case Study

On her way to school one morning, my daughter-in-law saw a car hit an elderly pedestrian. Although several drivers stopped to dial emergency services, no one except the man at fault braved pouring rain to help the injured woman. As a teacher, Cheri felt responsible for her students and faced possible reprimand for arriving late. Yet the woman's need compelled Cheri to stay at the scene, shielding the woman from rain until an ambulance arrived. What circumstances have prompted similar responses from you? What factors determine how you choose to give or withhold help from people in need?

Questions

1. Why do you think Mordecai advised Esther to hide her Jewish identity?

2. Have you ever been at the mercy of circumstances that fell beyond your control? How difficult was it to keep your focus on God and trust his sovereignty? In what ways did God reveal his presence and care through that experience, and how did it affect your ability to trust him in subsequent situations?

3. Esther was not immediately willing to risk her life for her people, but her faith helped overcome her reluctance. What role does faith play in your decisions to help others?

4. What factors make it difficult to offer help to some people? How might you address those challenges?

5. Consider the people who fall within your circle of influence. To what extent do your words, actions, attitudes, and choices impact their view of God? What steps might you take to strengthen your personal life witness?

NOTES

1. Karen H. Jobes, *Esther, The NIV Application Commentary* (Grand Rapids: Zondervan, 1999), 112–113.

FOCAL TEXT

Nehemiah 2:1–5; 5:1–13

BACKGROUND

Nehemiah 1—5

LESSON FIFTEEN

Nehemiah:
STANDING UP FOR PEOPLE

MAIN IDEA

Nehemiah demonstrated unselfish concern for his people in returning to Jerusalem to rebuild the wall and in calling for justice for the needy.

QUESTION TO EXPLORE

What does God want us to do when we see needs to be met?

STUDY AIM

To summarize how Nehemiah responded to the needs he saw and to identify ways in which God is challenging me to meet people's needs

QUICK READ

Responding to his people's desperate need, Nehemiah left his comfortable life to take on the difficult tasks of rebuilding Jerusalem's walls and of confronting social and economic oppression of its poor.

During a two-week visit with my in-laws, we heard that a dear cousin had also arrived from out-of-town. We hurried to our aunt's house to see him, but the joy of greeting quickly turned to sadness when we learned that he had come home for major heart surgery. The prognosis was grim. His heart was so damaged that doctors could not guarantee he would even survive the operation. The news cast a shadow over the rest of our visit, and our spirits ached as we prayed for God's healing intervention. It turned out to be God's plan for our cousin to enter glory. He did not survive surgery and now lives in the Lord's presence.

When bad news follows good, the abruptness of sorrow can be intensified by its contrast with previous joy. This was the case with Nehemiah. His gladness on seeing his brother was tempered by hearing sad news. The difficult plight of repatriated Jewish exiles living in Judah needn't have bothered him, since he was removed from the situation by hundreds of miles. But he took their need as his concern and made it a priority that disrupted his comfortable life in the Persian court.

Nehemiah 2:1–5

[1] In the month of Nisan in the twentieth year of King Artaxerxes, when wine was brought for him, I took the wine and gave it to the king. I had not been sad in his presence

before; **2** so the king asked me, "Why does your face look so sad when you are not ill? This can be nothing but sadness of heart."

I was very much afraid, **3** but I said to the king, "May the king live forever! Why should my face not look sad when the city where my fathers are buried lies in ruins, and its gates have been destroyed by fire?"

4 The king said to me, "What is it you want?"

Then I prayed to the God of heaven, **5** and I answered the king, "If it pleases the king and if your servant has found favor in his sight, let him send me to the city in Judah where my fathers are buried so that I can rebuild it."

NEHEMIAH 5:1–13

1 Now the men and their wives raised a great outcry against their Jewish brothers. **2** Some were saying, "We and our sons and daughters are numerous; in order for us to eat and stay alive, we must get grain."

3 Others were saying, "We are mortgaging our fields, our vineyards and our homes to get grain during the famine."

4 Still others were saying, "We have had to borrow money to pay the king's tax on our fields and vineyards. **5** Although we are of the same flesh and blood as our countrymen and though our sons are as good as theirs, yet we have to subject our sons and daughters to slavery.

Some of our daughters have already been enslaved, but we are powerless, because our fields and our vineyards belong to others."

⁶ When I heard their outcry and these charges, I was very angry. ⁷ I pondered them in my mind and then accused the nobles and officials. I told them, "You are exacting usury from your own countrymen!" So I called together a large meeting to deal with them ⁸ and said: "As far as possible, we have bought back our Jewish brothers who were sold to the Gentiles. Now you are selling your brothers, only for them to be sold back to us!" They kept quiet, because they could find nothing to say.

⁹ So I continued, "What you are doing is not right. Shouldn't you walk in the fear of our God to avoid the reproach of our Gentile enemies? ¹⁰ I and my brothers and my men are also lending the people money and grain. But let the exacting of usury stop! ¹¹ Give back to them immediately their fields, vineyards, olive groves and houses, and also the usury you are charging them—the hundredth part of the money, grain, new wine and oil."

¹² "We will give it back," they said. "And we will not demand anything more from them. We will do as you say."

Then I summoned the priests and made the nobles and officials take an oath to do what they had promised. ¹³ I also shook out the folds of my robe and said, "In this way may God shake out of his house and possessions every man who does not keep this promise. So may such a man be shaken out and emptied!"

At this the whole assembly said, "Amen," and praised the LORD. And the people did as they had promised.

A Grieving Heart (2:1–2)

When his brother was among the group of men who arrived from Judah, Nehemiah must have been overjoyed to see him. As they visited, Nehemiah was anxious to hear news of the Jews who had decided to leave Babylon and return to their homeland (Nehemiah 1:2). Hanani's report was discouraging. The people had been unable to rebuild Jerusalem because of opposition and persecution (Neh.1:3). Even worse, the temple reconstruction had come to a halt.

For the Jews, the temple was not a mere symbol of national unity. Rather, it was the center of their entire religious identity, practice, and law. It was where people offered sacrifices to atone for their sins. When the temple was destroyed, the nation's religious life fell into chaos. Throughout the Exile in Babylon, there had been no opportunity to properly atone for sins. That explains the emphasis given to rebuilding the temple when the Jews returned to Judah after their captivity ended (see Ezra 1:3–5).

Nehemiah was deeply grieved by the state of affairs in Judah. His concern compelled him to intercede on behalf of his countrymen. He "mourned and fasted and prayed" before God (Neh. 1:4). Four months later, the mourning and fasting had left its mark, altering his body and face to the extent that the king noticed and expressed concern. His question alarmed Nehemiah. In ancient Persia, it was customary to express delight for serving the king by maintaining a cheerful countenance in his presence. Failure to do so implied discontent or disloyalty and might jeopardize a person's position or life. Nehemiah realized that his appearance and demeanor placed him in danger of punishment.

A Bold Choice (2:3–5)

My grandmother used to quote the old proverb, *in for a penny, in for a pound*. By that she meant that if we accepted a responsibility, our commitment should be wholehearted, holding nothing back. When Artaxerxes inquired about Nehemiah's health, Nehemiah's personal fears might have prompted him to answer cautiously. Instead, risking the king's wrath, he grabbed the chance to intercede on behalf of the Jews in Judah. For four months, Nehemiah had prayed for such an opportunity. When it came, he continued to seek God's guidance by praying for help in wording his request so as not to offend or anger the king.

During the Babylonian conquest, Jerusalem had earned a reputation as a rebellious city. The designation continued into the period of Persian domination and had already come before Artaxerxes himself (see Ezra 4:11–12). When presenting his petition, Nehemiah tactfully omitted Jerusalem's name and instead stressed the importance of familial duty. Many ancient cultures placed high value on showing reverence and respect for dead ancestors. The devastated graves in Jerusalem brought shame on the nation. Nehemiah was asking, in effect, for permission to remove his disgrace by restoring order to the city where his ancestors were buried.

Nehemiah's faith and devotion to God shine from this passage. He relied completely on the Lord's guidance in every area. He brought all his needs, whether large or small, before God. Nehemiah expected and looked for God's answers and acted with boldness when he perceived them.

From Bad to Worse (5:1–5)

Artaxerxes responded favorably to Nehemiah's request. Not only did he authorize the reconstruction work for Jerusalem, but he also allowed Nehemiah to use timber from the royal forests for the project. Nehemiah was grateful to God for answering his prayer and preparing the king's heart for his petition. But Nehemiah had not been idle as he waited for God's response. In anticipation of the Lord's provision, he had carefully planned his whole venture, giving much thought to every detail. Once he received permission to proceed, Nehemiah secured letters from the king that would invest him with authority and prevent any of Jerusalem's enemies from interfering with its restoration. He was prepared for any potential problems that might hinder his mission.

Problems did arise. When he arrived in Judah, the Jews there were receptive and cooperative. They entered into the work of rebuilding the walls without grumbling or complaining. Their neighbors, though, began actively opposing the restoration of Jerusalem's walls. What began as insults and ridicule quickly escalated into threats of violence against the workers and their families. Nehemiah posted a twenty-four hour armed guard around Jerusalem's perimeter, and rallied the people to faith in God's protection.

The work progressed, but new problems surfaced from an unexpected quarter. The entire province of Judah had been experiencing a growing economic crisis. It is likely that neighboring people groups had expressed their hostility for the Jews by interrupting local trade. In spite of reduced commerce, people were still required to meet Persian taxation demands. In an ironic twist, the poorest people were taxed most heavily. The Persians not only collected on the fields that produced crops but also on the harvests they yielded. The farmers were paying double charges, while the upper class owed nothing on any uncultivated land they owned. This contributed to widespread poverty among rural families. By the time they turned over the tax money and crop percentages to the Persian government, there was not enough left to feed their own children. This left them with no choice but to mortgage their farms and borrow money to pay both taxes and creditors. But exorbitant usury fees by their own countrymen who were wealthy plunged them more deeply into debt. Some were left with no choice but to sell their children into slavery, to work until the family's debt was paid. The distress of these people intensified until they cried out to Nehemiah for help.

A Righteous Response (5:6–13)

Nehemiah 5:8 seems to indicate that when the exiles returned from Babylon, they had pooled their resources to gain release for the Jews who had become enslaved to foreign creditors. Now the nation's poverty had again forced many families into debt and slavery, but this time to their own countrymen. Merchants, artisans, and other professionals who fell into the upper middle class, and even nobles and officials of higher rank, were guilty of the same oppression of the poor as that of their Gentile neighbors. They were seizing land, houses, and crops to settle debts from high interest rates that no borrower could ever hope to repay.

Nehemiah realized that the situation could undermine the stability of the entire nation. It had happened before. When social oppression reached its peak in the

Northern kingdom of Israel, God sent Assyrian conquerors in judgment (see Amos 2:6–7, 4:1–2). The issue of debt enslavement had also played a part in Judah's fall to the Babylonians (see Jeremiah 34:8–17). After serious thought, Nehemiah decided to deal with the problem aggressively. He assembled all the people and presented charges in a form similar to a legal indictment.

But Nehemiah was not concerned with bringing punishment against the guilty parties. Instead, his goal was to avoid God's punishment against the nation for repeating the sins of their forefathers. Nehemiah made an appeal for righteousness. He confronted the wrongdoers with their sin and urged them to right judgment and action. The result was genuine repentance. The oppressors not only agreed to stop the usury but also volunteered to return everything they had taken from their debtors.

Nehemiah was a man of deep faith. He honored the Lord, spent time in his presence, and obeyed his laws. This sensitivity to God influenced his worldview. Having experienced God's faithfulness in his own life, he could not turn his back on the suffering of those whom God loved. Nehemiah seemed to have had the ability to judge people and situations from God's perspective. This sensitivity to God's heart emboldened him to act on behalf of people in need. Like Esther before him, Nehemiah's faith enabled him to relinquish his own will to God's sovereignty, and so his life made a deep impact on the history of his people.

Make it Personal

Nehemiah was able to view people and circumstances from God's perspective because he spent enough time with the Lord to know the Lord's heart. This ability to see things from God's view inspired him with courage to follow God's will, even when it may have seemed difficult. It also helped him to love and to value people in the same way God does. When Nehemiah boldly responded to needs around him, he was not concerned with praise or reward; he was simply doing what God required him to do.

Responding to the Holy Spirit's prompting is easier when we have spent enough time with him to recognize his voice. And the more we relinquish our own agendas and desires in favor of God's will, the more we learn to trust his leading. Allowing the needs of others to become a behavioral indicator in your life may not come naturally, but choosing to be used as God's agent in your world can lead to maturing faith and become a source of continual joy.

Nehemiah's Situation

Nebuchadnezzar destroyed Jerusalem and transported most of the Jewish population to Babylon in 586 B.C. After the Persians conquered Babylon fifty years later, many exiles returned to Judah. Others had prospered in Babylon and decided to stay. Nehemiah's family was among these who decided to stay. His story takes place during the reign of Persian king Artaxerxes (also called Longimanus), the son of Xerxes by a wife who preceded Esther.

Artaxerxes's reign (465–424 B.C.) was plagued by revolts that threatened his administration's stability. To cultivate political loyalty, he followed examples set by his predecessors (see Daniel 6:1) by appointing individuals from the empire's various people groups to high-ranking government positions.

Since many Jewish families had become wealthy and influential, it is not surprising to hear that a Jew would hold such a highly honored position as cupbearer to the king. In this capacity, Nehemiah might have been in charge of the palace wine as well as handing cups of wine to Artaxerxes himself. This personal access to the king was an enviable privilege.

Case Study

When a typhoon devastated the Philippines, schools suspended classes until floods receded and roads became passable. Students from a Christian international school in Manila spent their time off wading through muck and debris to help total strangers clean their houses and yards. For over a week the teenagers shoveled mud, scrubbed oily film from walls, and hauled away ruined furniture and appliances. Others helped prepare hot meals and emergency aid kits that they distributed daily to hundreds of displaced families. To what extent are you willing to sacrifice time or comfort to represent Christ's love in the world?

QUESTIONS

1. Nehemiah's life was rooted in Persia. Why do you think the Jews' situation in Judah affected him so deeply? Why did he feel a need to personally do something about it, when he might have just hired other people or asked the king to appoint someone else for the job?

2. What do you think Nehemiah was trying to accomplish by spending four months in fasting and prayer? What effect might the fasting have had on his attitude and sensitivity to God's leading?

3. Has there ever been a time when you were confronted with a need that seemed too big for you to handle? How did it make you feel? Why do you think some people are willing to take on a large challenge, while others shrink from it?

4. How can you know whether God wants to use you to meet someone's need? What might be some indicators that God is leading you to respond to a particular need?

5. Is it wrong to do something for someone else if your heart is not completely willing, even if you believe it is what God wants from you? What steps might you take to change your attitude in such a case?

6. What if a need arose that you would sincerely like to address, but honestly lack the ability or resources to do so? What do you think God might require of you in that situation?

Our Next New Study

(Available for use beginning September 2011)

THE CORINTHIAN LETTERS:
Imperatives for an Imperfect Church

1 CORINTHIANS: REPORTS AND QUESTIONS

Lesson 1	Get Together	1 Corinthians 1:1–17; 3:1–4
Lesson 2	Live Morally in an Immoral World	1 Corinthians 5:1–13
Lesson 3	Be Christian, Whether Married or Single	1 Corinthians 7:1–17, 25–35
Lesson 4	Wrestle Wisely with Life's Gray Areas	1 Corinthians 8:1–13; 10:23–33
Lesson 5	Use Spiritual Gifts for the Shared Good	1 Corinthians 12:1–14; 12:27—13:3
Lesson 6	Affirm the Resurrection Hope	1 Corinthians 15:3–20, 35–44, 50–57

2 CORINTHIANS: RENEWING THE RELATIONSHIP

Lesson 7	Use Your Difficulties to Help Others	2 Corinthians 1:1–11
Lesson 8	Heal Strained Relationships	2 Corinthians 1:12—2:13

Lesson 9	Measure Ministry By the Right Standards	2 Corinthians 2:17—3:6; 4:1–6
Lesson 10	View Life from Eternity	2 Corinthians 4:7—5:10
Lesson 11	Get Motivated to Minister	2 Corinthians 5:11—6:2
Lesson 12	Become Generous in Giving	2 Corinthians 8:1–15; 9:7–8, 11–15
Lesson 13	Rely On God's Grace	2 Corinthians 12:1–10

Additional Future Adult Studies

The Gospel of Matthew: A Primer for Discipleship — For use beginning December 2011

Turn to God—In Deeds, Not Words (Isaiah, Hosea, Amos, Micah) — For use beginning March 2012

How to Order More Bible Study Materials

It's easy! Just fill in the following information. For additional Bible study materials available both in print and online, see www.baptistwaypress.org, or get a complete order form of available print materials—including Spanish materials—by calling 1-866-249-1799 or e-mailing baptistway@texasbaptists.org.

Title of item	Price	Quantity	Cost
This Issue:			
Profiles in Character—Study Guide (BWP001112)	$3.55		
Profiles in Character—Large Print Study Guide (BWP001113)	$4.25		
Profiles in Character—Teaching Guide (BWP001114)	$4.95		
Additional Issues Available:			
Growing Together in Christ—Study Guide (BWP001036)	$3.25		
Growing Together in Christ—Teaching Guide (BWP001038)	$3.75		
Living Faith in Daily Life—Study Guide (BWP001095)	$3.55		
Living Faith in Daily Life—Large Print Study Guide (BWP001096)	$3.95		
Living Faith in Daily Life—Teaching Guide (BWP001097)	$4.25		
Participating in God's Mission—Study Guide (BWP001077)	$3.55		
Participating in God's Mission—Large Print Study Guide (BWP001078)	$3.95		
Participating in God's Mission—Teaching Guide (BWP001079)	$3.95		
Genesis: People Relating to God—Study Guide (BWP001088)	$2.35		
Genesis: People Relating to God—Large Print Study Guide (BWP001089)	$2.75		
Genesis: People Relating to God—Teaching Guide (BWP001090)	$2.95		
Genesis 12—50: Family Matters—Study Guide (BWP000034)	$1.95		
Genesis 12—50: Family Matters—Teaching Guide (BWP000035)	$2.45		
Leviticus, Numbers, Deuteronomy—Study Guide (BWP000053)	$2.35		
Leviticus, Numbers, Deuteronomy—Large Print Study Guide (BWP000052)	$2.35		
Leviticus, Numbers, Deuteronomy—Teaching Guide (BWP000054)	$2.95		
1 and 2 Samuel—Study Guide (BWP000002)	$2.35		
1 and 2 Samuel—Large Print Study Guide (BWP000001)	$2.35		
1 and 2 Samuel—Teaching Guide (BWP000003)	$2.95		
1 and 2 Kings: Leaders and Followers—Study Guide (BWP001025)	$2.95		
1 and 2 Kings: Leaders and Followers Large Print Study Guide (BWP001026)	$3.15		
1 and 2 Kings: Leaders and Followers Teaching Guide (BWP001027)	$3.45		
Ezra, Haggai, Zechariah, Nehemiah, Malachi—Study Guide (BWP001071)	$3.25		
Ezra, Haggai, Zechariah, Nehemiah, Malachi—Large Print Study Guide (BWP001072)	$3.55		
Ezra, Haggai, Zechariah, Nehemiah, Malachi—Teaching Guide (BWP001073)	$3.75		
Job, Ecclesiastes, Habakkuk, Lamentations—Study Guide (BWP001016)	$2.75		
Job, Ecclesiastes, Habakkuk, Lamentations—Large Print Study Guide (BWP001017)	$2.85		
Job, Ecclesiastes, Habakkuk, Lamentations—Teaching Guide (BWP001018)	$3.25		
Psalms and Proverbs—Study Guide (BWP001000)	$2.75		
Psalms and Proverbs—Teaching Guide (BWP001002)	$3.25		
Matthew: Hope in the Resurrected Christ—Study Guide (BWP001066)	$3.25		
Matthew: Hope in the Resurrected Christ—Large Print Study Guide (BWP001067)	$3.55		
Matthew: Hope in the Resurrected Christ—Teaching Guide (BWP001068)	$3.75		
Mark: Jesus' Works and Words—Study Guide (BWP001022)	$2.95		
Mark: Jesus' Works and Words—Large Print Study Guide (BWP001023)	$3.15		
Mark: Jesus' Works and Words—Teaching Guide (BWP001024)	$3.45		
Jesus in the Gospel of Mark—Study Guide (BWP000066)	$1.95		
Jesus in the Gospel of Mark—Teaching Guide (BWP000067)	$2.45		
Luke: Journeying to the Cross—Study Guide (BWP000057)	$2.35		
Luke: Journeying to the Cross—Large Print Study Guide (BWP000056)	$2.35		
Luke: Journeying to the Cross—Teaching Guide (BWP000058)	$2.95		
The Gospel of John: Light Overcoming Darkness, Part One—Study Guide (BWP001104)	$3.55		
The Gospel of John: Light Overcoming Darkness, Part One—Large Print Study Guide (BWP001105)	$3.95		
The Gospel of John: Light Overcoming Darkness, Part One—Teaching Guide (BWP001106)	$4.50		
The Gospel of John: Light Overcoming Darkness, Part Two—Study Guide (BWP001109)	$3.55		
The Gospel of John: Light Overcoming Darkness, Part Two—Large Print Study Guide (BWP001110)	$3.95		
The Gospel of John: Light Overcoming Darkness, Part Two—Teaching Guide (BWP001111)	$4.50		
The Gospel of John: The Word Became Flesh—Study Guide (BWP001008)	$2.75		
The Gospel of John: The Word Became Flesh—Large Print Study Guide (BWP001009)	$2.85		
The Gospel of John: The Word Became Flesh—Teaching Guide (BWP001010)	$3.25		
Acts: Toward Being a Missional Church—Study Guide (BWP001013)	$2.75		
Acts: Toward Being a Missional Church—Large Print Study Guide (BWP001014)	$2.85		
Acts: Toward Being a Missional Church—Teaching Guide (BWP001015)	$3.25		
Romans: What God Is Up To—Study Guide (BWP001019)	$2.95		
Romans: What God Is Up To—Large Print Study Guide (BWP001020)	$3.15		
Romans: What God Is Up To—Teaching Guide (BWP001021)	$3.45		

Item	Price		
Galatians and 1&2 Thessalonians—Study Guide (BWP001080)	$3.55	_____	_____
Galatians and 1&2 Thessalonians—Large Print Study Guide (BWP001081)	$3.95	_____	_____
Galatians and 1&2 Thessalonians—Teaching Guide (BWP001082)	$3.95	_____	_____
Ephesians, Philippians, Colossians—Study Guide (BWP001060)	$3.25	_____	_____
Ephesians, Philippians, Colossians—Large Print Study Guide (BWP001061)	$3.55	_____	_____
Ephesians, Philippians, Colossians—Teaching Guide (BWP001062)	$3.75	_____	_____
1, 2 Timothy, Titus, Philemon—Study Guide (BWP000092)	$2.75	_____	_____
1, 2 Timothy, Titus, Philemon—Teaching Guide (BWP000093)	$3.25	_____	_____
Letters of James and John—Study Guide (BWP001101)	$3.55	_____	_____
Letters of James and John—Large Print Study Guide (BWP001102)	$3.95	_____	_____
Letters of James and John—Teaching Guide (BWP001103)	$4.25	_____	_____
Revelation—Study Guide (BWP000084)	$2.35	_____	_____
Revelation—Large Print Study Guide (BWP000083)	$2.35	_____	_____
Revelation—Teaching Guide (BWP000085)	$2.95	_____	_____

Coming for use beginning September 2011

Item	Price		
The Corinthian Letters—Study Guide (BWP001121)	$3.55	_____	_____
The Corinthian Letters—Large Print Study Guide (BWP001122)	$4.25	_____	_____
The Corinthian Letters—Teaching Guide (BWP001123)	$4.95	_____	_____

Standard (UPS/Mail) Shipping Charges*			
Order Value	Shipping charge**	Order Value	Shipping charge**
$.01—$9.99	$6.50	$160.00—$199.99	$22.00
$10.00—$19.99	$8.00	$200.00—$249.99	$26.00
$20.00—$39.99	$9.00	$250.00—$299.99	$28.00
$40.00—$59.99	$10.00	$300.00—$349.99	$32.00
$60.00—$79.99	$11.00	$350.00—$399.99	$40.00
$80.00—$99.99	$12.00	$400.00—$499.99	$48.00
$100.00—$129.99	$14.00	$500.00—$599.99	$58.00
$130.00—$159.99	$18.00	$600.00—$799.99	$70.00**

Cost of items (Order value) _____

Shipping charges (see chart*) _____

TOTAL _____

*Plus, applicable taxes for individuals and other taxable entities (not churches) within Texas will be added. Please call 1-866-249-1799 if the exact amount is needed prior to ordering.

**For order values $800.00 and above, please call 1-866-249-1799 or check www.baptistwaypress.org

Please allow three weeks for standard delivery. For express shipping service: Call 1-866-249-1799 for information on additional charges.

YOUR NAME _____ PHONE _____

YOUR CHURCH _____ DATE ORDERED _____

SHIPPING ADDRESS _____

CITY _____ STATE _____ ZIP CODE _____

E-MAIL _____

MAIL this form with your check for the total amount to
BAPTISTWAY PRESS, Baptist General Convention of Texas,
333 North Washington, Dallas, TX 75246-1798
(Make checks to "Baptist Executive Board.")

OR, **FAX** your order anytime to: 214-828-5376, and we will bill you.

OR, **CALL** your order toll-free: 1-866-249-1799
(M-Fri 8:30 a.m.-5:00 p.m. central time), and we will bill you.

OR, **E-MAIL** your order to our internet e-mail address:
baptistway@texasbaptists.org, and we will bill you.

OR, **ORDER ONLINE** at www.baptistwaypress.org.

We look forward to receiving your order! Thank you!